THE BRIDGE BOOK

VOLUME 4 — DEFENSE AT CONTRACT BRIDGE

by Frank Stewart and Randall Baron

Drawings by Jude Goodwin

Published by
Devyn Press, Inc.
Louisville,
Kentucky

Dedications

To C. H.
F. S.

To Mary, Devyn and Dustin.
R. S. B.

Acknowledgments

Grateful thanks to:
Betty Mattision for her patience and typesetting skills;
Pat Houington, Tony Lipka and Henry Francis for their editorial
   assistance;
Izzy Ellis and V.B.I. for their cover photography;
also to Mimi Maier, and Bonnie Baron Pollack.

Players are referred to as "he" to make the text more readable.

Printed in the United States of America.

Devyn Press, Inc.
3600 Chamberlain Lane, Suite 230
Louisville, KY 40241

ISBN 0-910791-56-2

Table of Contents

Preface

To beat a close contract with a well-conceived defense is one of the biggest thrills in bridge.

This book, the fourth in a multi-volume series, is a guide to good defensive play. Many basic texts shortchange defense — surprising, since it is a tough subject. It is on defense that the aspiring player must begin to think for himself, to reason, to count, to reconstruct the concealed hands. Clear and logical thought is essential. This book will help you develop the right thought processes, in addition to providing a review of the basic defensive skills.

To get the most from this book, we suggest that you try to answer the questions in the text (posed in boldface) before reading on. Each chapter ends with a summary, plus quizzes so you may test your understanding of the material.

Since actual play has no substitute as a learning experience, we advise you to play bridge as much as possible. We also encourage you to read other books (many published by Devyn Press) and check out the bridge column in your local newspaper.

The rewards of mastering this game are most satisfying. You will have a stimulating way of entertaining yourself and a way of making friends wherever you go. If you are more ambitious, organized tournament competition can lead to a world championship! Good luck. Enjoy yourself.

Chapter 1

COUNT YOUR TRICKS!
DEFENDING ON AN ASSUMPTION

Bridge is a game of problem-solving, and you'll have a lot of problems to solve in this book. Let's start with a tough defensive problem to get your brain in gear.

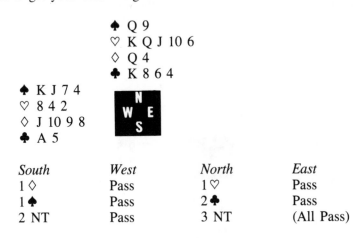

	♠ Q 9		
	♡ K Q J 10 6		
	◊ Q 4		
	♣ K 8 6 4		

♠ K J 7 4
♡ 8 4 2
◊ J 10 9 8
♣ A 5

South	West	North	East
1 ◊	Pass	1 ♡	Pass
1 ♠	Pass	2 ♣	Pass
2 NT	Pass	3 NT	(All Pass)

Get into the habit of remembering the bidding and absorbing what it tells you about the opponents' holdings. *Inferences* from the bidding are always available. So too are *negative* inferences from what the opponents do *not* bid. Listening to the bidding may help you plan the defense.

You, West, lead the ◊ J against 3 NT. Declarer studies dummy for a while and plays the ◊ Q, which wins. Next, declarer leads a club from dummy and plays the queen from his hand. Suppose you win this trick. **What do you lead next?**

What do you know about declarer's hand? He surely has the ◊ A and ◊ K. Partner would have helped by playing one of those cards if he could. Declarer holds the ♣ Q — that card you saw. How about hearts? **Who has the ♡ A?** To answer, put yourself in declarer's place. How would you play this hand if you lacked the ♡ A? What suit would you lead right away? *Hearts!* Declarer has neglected to establish his best suit only because it is already established! He can cash five heart tricks whenever he wants. He also has three tricks with high diamonds, and dummy's ♣K is worth a trick. That's nine tricks! He will make the contract unless you take four more tricks right now. **What card must partner have?** The ♠A, right? **How do you handle the spade suit?** The layout might be:

```
              ♠ Q 9
♠ K J 7 4     ■         ♠ A 8 3
              ♠ 10 6 5 2
```

Now the only way to take four tricks is to lead the king first. Partner will *unblock* his 8, getting out of the way. Then you lead a low spade to partner's ace, and the spade return goes through declarer's 10-6 to your J-7. Four tricks. The full deal is:

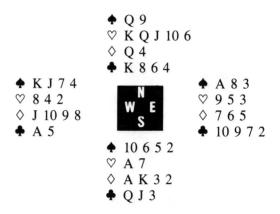

```
                ♠ Q 9
                ♡ K Q J 10 6
                ◇ Q 4
                ♣ K 8 6 4
♠ K J 7 4                        ♠ A 8 3
♡ 8 4 2         N                ♡ 9 5 3
◇ J 10 9 8    W   E              ◇ 7 6 5
♣ A 5           S                ♣ 10 9 7 2
                ♠ 10 6 5 2
                ♡ A 7
                ◇ A K 3 2
                ♣ Q J 3
```

Note that declarer would have opened *1 NT* with the ♠A in addition to his other values.

This is a tough deal. To defend it correctly, you must draw an inference from declarer's play, count his tricks, handle a card combination correctly, and assume that partner has the ace of a suit declarer bid so your side will have a chance for five tricks! These are some of the things this book will teach you — things that will make you a demon defender.

Let's go further into one of the concepts just seen. You needed five tricks to beat 3 NT, and there was only one way to get them. Just as a good declarer counts his winners in planning the play, the defenders should try to *count their potential tricks*. Counting tricks on defense may tell you what you must do to set the contract. Frequently, if you ask yourself, "Where is the setting trick coming from?'' there will be only one possible answer. Here is a simple example:

1.

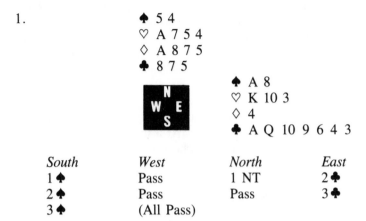

	♠ 5 4	
	♡ A 7 5 4	
	◊ A 8 7 5	
	♣ 8 7 5	
		♠ A 8
		♡ K 10 3
		◊ 4
		♣ A Q 10 9 6 4 3

South	West	North	East
1 ♠	Pass	1 NT	2 ♣
2 ♠	Pass	Pass	3 ♣
3 ♠	(All Pass)		

West leads the ♣2, and declarer follows with the jack on your ace. **How do you defend?**

Partner has led a singleton club, and you can give him a ruff. The trump ace will be a third trick, and the ♡K offers a good chance for a fourth. The best chance for the setting trick is a *diamond ruff*. But partner's only entry to give you that ruff may be his club ruff. So you must return your singleton diamond at trick two.

Declarer will win and lead a trump. You take your ace, give partner his club ruff and receive a diamond ruff in return. Perhaps your ♡K will score (or maybe partner will turn up with a trick.)

2.

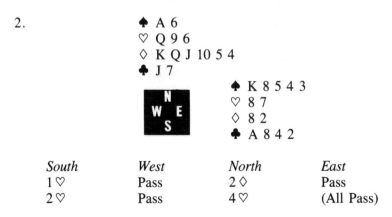

	♠ A 6	
	♡ Q 9 6	
	◊ K Q J 10 5 4	
	♣ J 7	
		♠ K 8 5 4 3
		♡ 8 7
		◊ 8 2
		♣ A 8 4 2

South	West	North	East
1 ♡	Pass	2 ◊	Pass
2 ♡	Pass	4 ♡	(All Pass)

West leads the ♠Q. Declarer wins dummy's ace and leads the

♡ Q, losing a finesse to partner's king. Now partner leads the ♠ 10.
How do you defend?

Declarer must have the ◊ A as part of his opening bid, so you'll
need *two clubs tricks* in addition to partner's trump king and a spade.
Overtake the ♠ 10 and lead a *low* club. If partner has the ♣K, you
take two tricks with no problem. But if declarer holds the ♣K and
partner the *queen* you may still get two tricks. Declarer may guess
wrong on your club lead and play *low*.

(As this deal shows, it is easiest to count defensive tricks when
the contract is a game or slam. Your options will be limited when
declarer has most of the high cards. At a low partscore, you may
have to wait for the play to develop before your source of tricks is
clear.)

3.

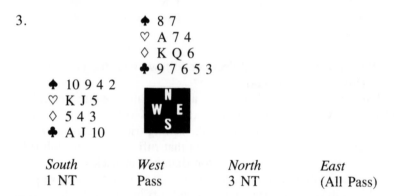

| ♠ 8 7 |
| ♡ A 7 4 |
| ◊ K Q 6 |
| ♣ 9 7 6 5 3 |

♠ 10 9 4 2
♡ K J 5
◊ 5 4 3
♣ A J 10

South	*West*	*North*	*East*
1 NT	Pass	3 NT	(All Pass)

You lead the ♠2. Partner wins the ace, on which declarer follows
with the jack. Partner's return of the ♠3 is won by declarer's queen.
Declarer then leads the ♣K to your ace. **What do you lead?**

You can return a spade at this point and establish a long card, but
you won't beat the contract. Count your tricks: a club, a second club
that declarer will give you and two spades. To have a chance for
five tricks, you must shift to a heart, hoping partner has the ♡ Q.

The full deal is:

```
                  ♠ 8 7
                  ♡ A 7 4
                  ◇ K Q 6
                  ♣ 9 7 6 5 3
  ♠ 10 9 4 2                    ♠ A 6 5 3
  ♡ K J 5          N            ♡ Q 10 3
  ◇ 5 4 3        W   E          ◇ 9 7 2
  ♣ A J 10         S            ♣ 8 4 2
                  ♠ K Q J
                  ♡ 9 8 6 2
                  ◇ A J 10 8
                  ♣ K Q
```

If partner is allowed to win his ♡ Q, he will switch back to spades and set up the setting trick. You can see how counting your tricks can keep you from adopting a hopeless line of defense.

4.

          ♠ A K
          ♡ Q 9 7
          ◇ 7 6 5
          ♣ K J 10 8 7

                             ♠ Q 10 4 3
        N   ♡ A
   W   **E**   ◇ 9 8 4
        S   ♣ A 9 6 5 4

South	West	North	East
1 ♡	Pass	2 ♣	Pass
2 ♡	Pass	4 ♡	(All Pass)

West leads the ♣2. You win the ace, and declarer follows low. Partner has led another singleton and you can give him a club ruff, but have you counted your tricks? **How do you defend?**

Three tricks are easy to see. The fourth trick almost surely must come from diamonds. **What must partner hold in diamonds to set this contract?** The ace or king. If declarer has both cards, he will have time to draw trumps and throw away any diamond losers on dummy's clubs. If partner has the ◇ A, there will be no problem. But suppose he has the ◇ K behind declarer's A-Q. **Do you see what will happen if you return a club and give partner his club ruff immediately?** Partner can't lead a diamond from his king, so declarer will have time to knock out the trump ace, draw trumps and throw his diamond losers on the clubs.

To give yourself the best chance for four tricks, return a diamond at trick two. If partner's diamond trick is the king, you must lead a diamond *through* declarer early, setting up partner's king while you still control the trump suit. Note that giving partner his club ruff can wait, since you have the trump ace as a sure reentry.

In some of our problem deals, you had to *assume* that partner had a certain holding to have a chance on defense. (In the last deal, for example, you had to give partner a high diamond, else the contract would surely make.) This concept, called *defending on an assumption*, is the second important idea in this chapter.

It pays to be an optimist on defense. You should always try to imagine a hand for declarer, consistent with the bidding, that will let you defeat him. If declarer has a different hand and the contract is cold, shrug it off and go on to the next deal. You just don't want declarer to make his contract when you have a way to set him.

Here is a simple example of defending on an assumption:

5.
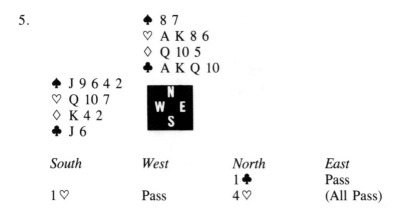

South	West	North	East
		1♣	Pass
1♡	Pass	4♡	(All Pass)

You lead the ♣4. Partner plays the king, losing to declarer's ace. Declarer then cashes the A-K of trumps, partner following once, and begins to run dummy's club suit. **How do you defend?**

You have one certain trick in hearts, but no tricks in clubs and none in spades either, since partner's play of the ♠K marks declarer with the queen. So your options are limited. Needing three diamond tricks, you must find partner with the ace and jack. Ruff in with your trump queen quickly, since declarer will discard some of his diamonds on dummy's clubs, and lead a diamond.

On many deals the defenders will see only a slim chance of defeating the contract. There may be just one hand for declarer that will allow the contract to be set. Thus, the defenders' task is simple. They assume that the desired lie of the cards actually exists.

6.

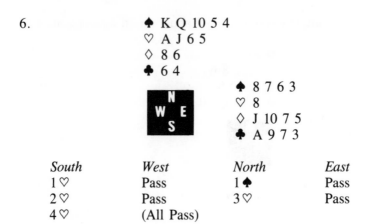

♠ K Q 10 5 4
♡ A J 6 5
◊ 8 6
♣ 6 4

♠ 8 7 6 3
♡ 8
◊ J 10 7 5
♣ A 9 7 3

South	West	North	East
1 ♡	Pass	1 ♠	Pass
2 ♡	Pass	3 ♡	Pass
4 ♡	(All Pass)		

Partner leads a low trump. Declarer wins and draws another round. He then leads the ♠J from hand, and partner wins the ace. He leads a club to your ace. **What do you return?**

You need four tricks. Partner must hold either (1) the ♣K and the ◊A, or (2) the ◊A and ◊Q (or, far less likely, the A-K). In both cases you need to return a *diamond*. A club return works in the first case but not the second. (A good partner would lead the ♣K here if he had it, to make things easier on you. This is another argument for a diamond return.)

7.

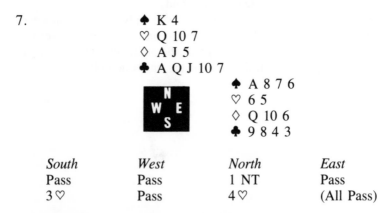

♠ K 4
♡ Q 10 7
◊ A J 5
♣ A Q J 10 7

♠ A 8 7 6
♡ 6 5
◊ Q 10 6
♣ 9 8 4 3

South	West	North	East
Pass	Pass	1 NT	Pass
3 ♡	Pass	4 ♡	(All Pass)

West leads the ♠J. Declarer puts up dummy's king, and you win the ace. **What do you lead at trick two?**

Let's make some *assumptions*. If declarer has solid trumps, he will always make his game, probably with overtricks. So the first assumption is that partner has a trump trick. Declarer is marked with the ♠ Q from partner's lead of the jack, so the defense has no further spade tricks. No club tricks are available either. Even if declarer lacks the ♣ K, he can take a winning finesse. So two tricks must come from diamonds. That means partner must hold the ◇ K — and the defenders certainly need to lead diamonds *quickly*, before declarer can draw trumps and take the clubs for diamond discards. As the only chance, then, switch to a low diamond at trick two. If declarer's hand is:

♠ Q 5
♡ A J 9 4 3
◇ 8 4 3 2
♣ K 5

you can set him. You therefore *assume* that declarer has such a hand.

8.

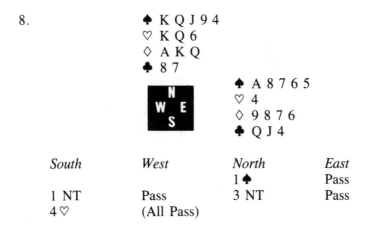

	♠ K Q J 9 4		
	♡ K Q 6		
	◇ A K Q		
	♣ 8 7		

♠ A 8 7 6 5
♡ 4
◇ 9 8 7 6
♣ Q J 4

South	West	North	East
		1 ♠	Pass
1 NT	Pass	3 NT	Pass
4 ♡	(All Pass)		

West leads the ♠ 2. Dummy plays low, and you take your ace, declarer following with the 3. **How do you defend?**

This deal is more complicated. Three key honors are missing, and if your partner has *any two* of them, you will always beat the contract at least one trick. (Suppose, for example, that partner holds the ♡ A and the ♣ K. You can either give him his spade ruff right away, after which a club shift will set up a trick that he cashes when he wins his ace of trumps; or you can shift to the ♣ Q at trick two; he puts you in with your ♣ J when he wins his trump trick, and now you give him his spade ruff.)

But say that partner has only *one* of the three key honors. If he has the ♡ A, the best you can do is to hold the contract to *four* with

13

a spade ruff. If he has the ♣K, a spade ruff is necessary to hold it to *five!* If he has the ♣A . . . Aha! We've found a time where your play matters. Suppose declarer's hand is:

♠ 10 3
♡ A J 9 7 5 3
◊ 5 4
♣ K 10 3

Now you must return the ♣Q to get all your tricks. Give partner his spade ruff prematurely and you'll never be in again to come through declarer's ♣K. Partner will have to cash his ♣A to stop an overtrick.

Since this hand is the only one where your play makes a difference, return the ♣Q.

9.

♠ A K J
♡ Q J 7 6
◊ Q
♣ K Q J 8 7

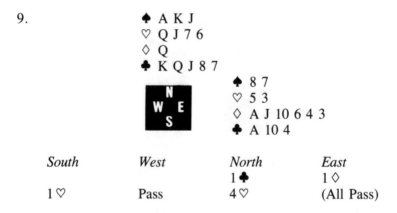

♠ 8 7
♡ 5 3
◊ A J 10 6 4 3
♣ A 10 4

South	West	North	East
		1 ♣	1 ◊
1 ♡	Pass	4 ♡	(All Pass)

West leads the ◊ 8, and you take your ace. **What do you lead at trick two?**

Again, partner must have the ace or king of trumps for the defenders to have a chance. His presumed trump trick and your two aces will make the defensive book. **Where can the setting trick come from?** It looks as if the only hope is to give partner a *club ruff.* He is unlikely to have a singleton club, since he probably would have led it instead of a diamond. But he may have a *doubleton.* In that case, you must lead a *low* club at trick two, keeping communication open. When partner wins his trump trick, he can return his other club. You win it and give him his ruff.

To finish our discussion, here is a beautiful hand on which East made a fine play based on counting tricks and defending on an assumption.

10.

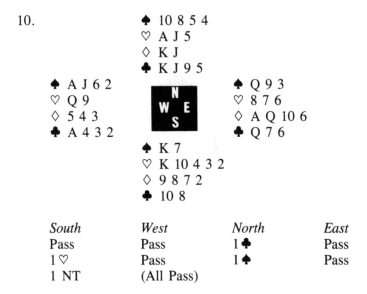

♠ 10 8 5 4
♡ A J 5
◊ K J
♣ K J 9 5

♠ A J 6 2
♡ Q 9
◊ 5 4 3
♣ A 4 3 2

♠ Q 9 3
♡ 8 7 6
◊ A Q 10 6
♣ Q 7 6

♠ K 7
♡ K 10 4 3 2
◊ 9 8 7 2
♣ 10 8

South	*West*	*North*	*East*
Pass	Pass	1♣	Pass
1♡	Pass	1♠	Pass
1 NT	(All Pass)		

West led the ♠2. Declarer played low from dummy, and East put in the *9,* a good start for the defense. (East thought declarer was likely to have the ♠A or ♠K, so playing the queen would give declarer a second stopper in dummy. East hoped the 9 would force out declarer's high card.)

After winning his ♠K, declarer led a heart to the jack, cashed the ♡A and continued hearts. On the fourth heart East had to plan his defense. His reasoning: "Declarer has five heart tricks and one spade, so if he has the ♣A or the ♠A, he is home. I must assume partner has both of those cards. Then we can take three spade tricks (East knew his partner held the ♠J when the 9 forced the king at trick one), three diamonds and the ♣A. Can anything go wrong? Yes, partner doesn't know I have the diamonds sewed up. He may *duck* his ♣A when declarer leads a club toward dummy, and declarer will take his seventh trick with the king. Well, I can prevent that."

On the fourth heart East discarded his ♣Q! Now West had no reason to duck his ♣A, since declarer no longer had a guess. The defenders cashed their seven tricks. Full marks to East for using his imagination, plus the techniques of assumption and counting defensive tricks.

15

To review:

In this chapter you learned two simple but important concepts that apply in almost every deal you defend:

I. COUNT YOUR TRICKS ON DEFENSE. Counting possible winners may tell you what you must do to set the contract.

II. DEFEND ON AN ASSUMPTION. To count enough tricks to set the contract, you must often *assume* that partner or declarer has a specific holding.

QUIZ ON COUNTING DEFENSIVE TRICKS AND DEFENDING ON AN ASSUMPTION

1.

♠ A K 8 6
♡ 8 6
◇ Q 8 5
♣ A K Q J

♠ Q 10 5
♡ J 9 7 5 2
◇ K 7 3
♣ 10 7

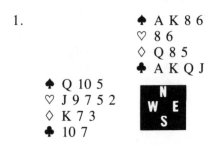

North opened 1♣, South responded 1♠, North raised to 4♠. You lead the ♡5. Partner plays the king, and declarer wins the ace. Declarer cashes the ♠A and ♠K, partner following once, and then begins to run dummy's clubs. How do you defend?

2.

♠ K Q 10 8 4
♡ Q 7 6
◇ 6 5
♣ K Q 4

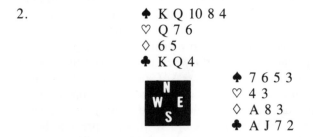

♠ 7 6 5 3
♡ 4 3
◇ A 8 3
♣ A J 7 2

South opened 1♡, North responded 1♠. South rebid 2♡, North raised to 4♡. West leads the ◇2. How do you defend?

3.

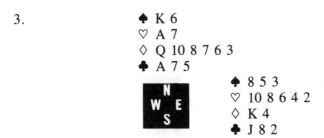

♠ K 6
♡ A 7
◇ Q 10 8 7 6 3
♣ A 7 5

      ♠ 8 5 3
      ♡ 10 8 6 4 2
      ◇ K 4
      ♣ J 8 2

North opened 1 ◇, South responded 2 NT, North raised to 3 NT. West leads the ♣Q. Declarer takes dummy's king and leads a low diamond. How do you defend?

4.

♠ K 6
♡ A K 6
◇ K Q 10 4
♣ Q 7 6 5

♠ 10 9 8 4
♡ 9 8 5
◇ A 7 2
♣ K J 10

North opened 1 NT, South responded 3 ♡, North raised to 4 ♡. You lead the ♠ 10. Dummy's king wins. Declarer plays the ace, king and queen of trumps, partner following twice with low cards. Declarer then tables the ◇J. How do you defend?

5.

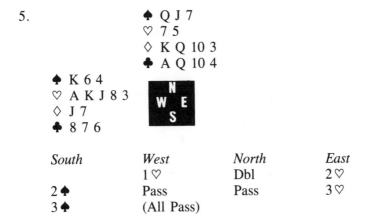

♠ Q J 7
♡ 7 5
◇ K Q 10 3
♣ A Q 10 4

♠ K 6 4
♡ A K J 8 3
◇ J 7
♣ 8 7 6

South	West	North	East
	1 ♡	Dbl	2 ♡
2 ♣	Pass	Pass	3 ♡
3 ♣	(All Pass)		

You lead the ♡A and continue with the ♡K. Declarer follows low to both tricks. How do you continue?

6.

♠ K J
♡ A J 9 4
◇ A Q J 7
♣ 8 7 6

♠ Q 6 5 4
♡ K 6 3
◇ 6 5 4
♣ A K 5

North opened 1 NT, South responded 3 ♡, North raised to 4 ♡. West leads the ♠ 10. You cover dummy's jack, and declarer wins the ace. At trick two declarer passes the ♡ Q to your king. How do you defend?

7.

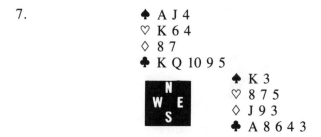

♠ A J 4
♡ K 6 4
◇ 8 7
♣ K Q 10 9 5

♠ K 3
♡ 8 7 5
◇ J 9 3
♣ A 8 6 4 3

South opened 1 ♠, North responded 2 ♣. South rebid 2 NT, North tried 3 ♠, South bid 4 ♠. West leads the ♣2, and declarer follows low. How do you defend?

8.

♠ 7 6
♡ J 10 7 6
◇ A Q 10 5
♣ K Q J

♠ A 9 4 2
♡ K Q 4
◇ 6
♣ 10 8 6 5 3

South opened 1 ♡, North responded 3 ♡, South went on to 4 ♡. West leads the ♠K. How do you defend?

SOLUTIONS

1. West must ruff in on the third club and shift to diamonds (preferably by leading the king and another). Declarer is marked with the ♡Q from East's play of the king, so the defenders need three diamonds tricks. If West doesn't use his trump queen immediately, declarer will discard a diamond on the clubs.

2. Win the ◊A and shift to a *low* club. To take four tricks, you must find partner with either the ♠A or a trump trick — if he has neither, declarer will make five. Partner also needs the ♣10 (the 9 may do, if declarer misguesses); or, if partner has a high trump, any doubleton club. You hope to take the ◊A, partner's presumed trick, the ♣A, and either another club trick or a club ruff.

3. Play the ◊K, hoping to return a spade and establish partner's suit while he retains the ◊A as an entry. If declarer holds the ◊A, you won't beat the contract. Be an optimist!

4. Take the ◊A and lead your ♣K and ♣J. You must assume that partner has the ♣A. Perhaps you can take a diamond trick and three clubs.

5. To beat this contract, you must assume that partner has an ace. In that case, you can get a diamond ruff. Lead the ◊J at trick three. If declarer wins the ◊A and leads a trump toward dummy, you must jump in with your king and lead your other diamond. When partner wins the trump ace later, he returns a diamond, giving you a ruff with your last low trump. If partner's ace is in diamonds, he'll have to guess to duck the first round of diamonds, keeping communication with your hand.

6. Your only hope is to take three club tricks. Lead a *low* club from your A-K! If declarer has Q-10-x, he will probably play the 10, losing to partner's jack.

7. You can count three tricks: the ♣A, a club ruff and the ♠K. If partner has a red ace, the contract will be defeated easily. If he does not have an ace, however, he will need the ◊K. In that case, you must lead a diamond at trick two, setting up partner's king while you still control trumps. The club ruff can wait, since you have a trump reentry. How do you know that partner has the ◊K? You don't, but that is the only time your play matters. You thus defend on the assumption that he holds the king.

8. You have two spade tricks and a trump trick. There will be no tricks in clubs or diamonds — declarer must have the ♣A

19

and ◇ K for his opening bid — so the setting trick must come from trumps. Overtake the ♠K and lead your singleton diamond. When declarer leads a trump from dummy, you *split your honors,* win the second trump and lead to partner's ♠Q so he can give you a diamond ruff.

Chapter 2

BASIC IDEAS IN DEFENSIVE PLAY

Early in the play, before the defenders know much about the deal and have little idea what strategy they should adopt, they play according to *general principles*. The concepts in this chapter are only principles or tendencies. Too many exceptional cases exist for you to regard them as inviolable rules.

I. *CHOOSING A CARD TO LEAD*

The Basics:
Once you choose a *suit* to lead, the *card* you select from that suit is usually a matter of convention.

1. If your suit contains a *sequence*, lead the *top* card in your sequence. From this holding, for example:

K Q J 7 5

lead the *king*. It makes sense to lead *one* of your high cards, which forces declarer to spend the ace if he has it; the king is led so your partner will know what your holding is.

> A SEQUENCE CONSISTS OF THREE OR MORE CARDS THAT ARE TOUCHING IN RANK, THE HIGHEST ONE OF WHICH IS AN HONOR.

Therefore, this holding:

Q 9 8 7 4

does *not* contain a sequence. But these holdings:

K Q *10* 5
J 10 *8*

which have *two* equals, *plus* a nearby spot card, are treated like true sequences — you still lead the top card. Most players, in fact, would lead the king *against a suit contract* from:

$$\text{K Q 7 5 3}$$

to *assure* a chance for *one* trick.

These holdings:

$$\text{Q 10 9 8 5}$$
$$\text{K J 10 8 5}$$

contain *interior* sequences. Lead the top card *in the sequence.*

2. If your suit barely lacks a sequential holding:

$$\text{Q J 6 4 2}$$

or if it is completely ragged:

$$\text{Q 10 8 4 2}$$

the traditional lead is *the fourth-highest* card in your suit. You might as well lead *low* from a broken holding, since you hope partner can contribute a helpful card. The lead of the *fourth-highest* card is not an arbitrary selection, but one that, again, sends helpful information to your partner. If, for example, you are defending a notrump con-

BUILD YOUR DEFENSIVE KNOWLEDGE BY LEARNING THE IMPORTANT PRINCIPLES.

tract, and your partner leads the ♡2, you can assume he has led from a *four-card* heart suit.

Suppose you choose to lead from:

Q 8 6 4 2

You start with the *4*. The dummy has only low cards, partner plays the 10 and declarer wins the king. Later, you lead this suit again (expecting partner to hold the jack). Lead your *2* the second time, suggesting that your suit was *five* cards long originally.

3. Many players avoid leading fourth highest from a *worthless* suit. The lead of a *low* card somehow *implies strength* and it may induce your partner to return your suit when a switch to a different suit would be better. From this suit:

9 8 6 4 2

most players would lead their *highest* (or second-highest) *spot*, encouraging a switch if partner deemed it best.

From *three low* cards, experts do not agree on the proper card to lead. We suggest you lead high and play the middle card next.

4. From a *doubleton* (with one exception), lead the *top* card to get it out of the way.

5. What would you lead from this suit?

A J 7 5 3

This time it depends on the contract. Against *notrump*, lead the *fourth-highest* card. You may give up one trick, but you start to set up your long cards and you preserve communication with partner's hand. Against a *suit* contract, however, lead the ace if you lead the suit at all. *Avoid underleading aces* against a suit contract. Quite often, declarer will trump the second round of the suit, and you will never get your ace. The underlead of an ace may also mislead your partner and allow declarer to win an undeserved trick.

6. How about the lead from A-K?

A K 7 5 3

Again, you may be willing to lead *low* vs. notrump to keep communication. But you will certainly cash your top cards against a suit contract.

7. You will normally lead *low* from holdings such as Q-x-x or K-x-x-x in a suit partner bid. Beware the popular misconception that you always lead your *highest* card in partner's suit.

♡ 7 5

♡ Q 9 4   ■   ♡ K 10 6 3 2

♡ A J 8

South is declarer after East opened the bidding with 1 ♡. If West leads the *queen,* declarer gets two heart tricks; if West leads low, saving his queen, declarer is limited to one trick.

The Fine Points:

1. Returning partner's lead:

You return the lead of partner's suit with the idea of telling him *how many cards* he started with. Return your *highest* remaining card if you started with *three,* but your original *fourth*-highest card (as though you were leading the suit for the first time yourself) if you started with *more than three.* Suppose partner leads a spade. You win the ♠A and will lead the suit again. Return the *9* from

♠ A 9 4

and the *2* from

♠ A 8 5 2

2. As an exception, you may judge to lead *high from length* in partner's bid suit.

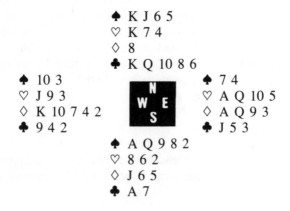

♠ K J 6 5
♡ K 7 4
◇ 8
♣ K Q 10 8 6

♠ 10 3   ♠ 7 4
♡ J 9 3   ♡ A Q 10 5
◇ K 10 7 4 2   ◇ A Q 9 3
♣ 9 4 2   ♣ J 5 3

♠ A Q 9 8 2
♡ 8 6 2
◇ J 6 5
♣ A 7

East opens 1 ◊, South overcalls 1 ♠ and North bids game in spades. West's normal lead is the ◊ 4. But if East wins the first trick, the best he can do is cash the ♡ A to hold declarer to five.

If West realizes that he will never be on lead again, he might make the excellent lead of the ◊ K, giving some flexibility to the defense — the defenders can choose who wins the first trick and leads to trick two. If West retains the lead, perhaps he can make an effective shift through dummy to partner's strength. In the actual case, West can shift to his ♡ J (hoping partner has A-Q-10; the defenders must take tricks in a hurry, since dummy's clubs are a threat for discards), and declarer will be down before he gets started!

3. The purpose of leading the *top* card of a doubleton is to *unblock* the suit if partner has honors or to tell him that you are *short* in the suit. You may ignore this principle if neither factor is a consideration. For example, lead low from a doubleton in *trumps*. If you lead the *10* of trumps from 10-x, you may waste a valuable card. (You may be able to use it to overruff declarer or dummy, for instance.) There is no reason to tell partner that you are short in *trumps*.

(Similarly, if you choose a trump lead from J-10-x, lead *low*. If you lead your jack, you may crash partner's singleton king or queen.) It may even be right to lead low from a doubleton honor.

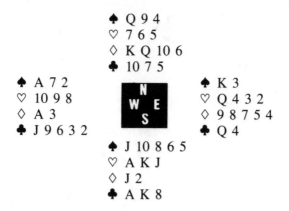

```
                    ♠ Q 9 4
                    ♡ 7 6 5
                    ◊ K Q 10 6
                    ♣ 10 7 5
     ♠ A 7 2                          ♠ K 3
     ♡ 10 9 8          N              ♡ Q 4 3 2
     ◊ A 3          W     E           ◊ 9 8 7 5 4
     ♣ J 9 6 3 2       S              ♣ Q 4
                    ♠ J 10 8 6 5
                    ♡ A K J
                    ◊ J 2
                    ♣ A K 8
```

South opens 1♠, North raises to 2♠, South jumps to 4♠. West leads the ♡ 10, won by declarer's king. Declarer leads a low spade to dummy's 9 and East's king. **What should East lead now?**

Suppose East decides to switch to a club, through dummy's weakness. If he leads the queen, declarer wins the ace or king and tables the ◊ J. West wins the second diamond but he can't continue the attack on clubs by leading from his jack (because the 10 is in dummy). Declarer then has time to give up the other high trump, draw trumps and discard his club loser on dummy's diamonds.

To beat this contract, East must lead his low club from Q-4! West can now continue clubs, setting up a trick when he gets in.

4. Suppose you lead from your spade sequence against a notrump contract in this situation:

```
                    ♠ 7 5 3
     ♠ K Q J 8 4       ■          ♠ A 9 6
                    ♠ 10 2
```

Your ♠K wins the first trick. (Partner, as we will see, plays his ♠9, an *encouraging* signal.) What card should you lead at trick two? These little details can make a big difference. If you continue with the queen, partner won't know what is going on. He may play low instead of getting his ace out of your way, fearing that you tried a spade lead from K-Q-x. Now you may not take all your tricks. Therefore, you should lead the ♠J at the second trick. Partner will know it is safe to play the ace, unblocking the suit. (Note that you can't risk leading *low* at your second turn. For all you know, partner's ♠9 is a singleton.)

IIa. SECOND-HAND PLAY

The Basics:
The tendency in second seat is to *wait*. When you are second to play, your partner plays last. You can usually avoid desperate tactics when your partner is so well placed. By adopting the strategy of playing low in second seat, you might make declarer guess what to play from his own hand or dummy in third position; force him to spend a high card to keep your partner from winning the trick cheaply; or avoid the embarrassment of crashing one of your high cards with one of partner's.

Sometimes, you can make it harder for declarer to establish his high cards. Look at this position:

```
              8 7 4
 J 9 5         ■          A 10 6 3
              K Q 2
```

Declarer leads this suit from dummy. If East takes his ace immediately, declarer plays low, saving his two winners. If East plays *low* on the first round, declarer wins one high card, but then he must find a way to reach dummy to lead toward the other high card. If entries to dummy are scarce, declarer may be hurt by East's *duck*.

Change the situation slightly:

```
              8 7 4
 Q 9 5 2       ■          A 10 6 3
              K J
```

Now, if East plays low as second hand, declarer must guess whether to play the king or jack from his hand. But if East grabs his ace, declarer's guess vanishes.

```
              K 7 5
 10 8 3        ■          A J 4
              Q 9 6 2
```

Declarer leads from dummy. If East plays the ace, declarer wins

27

three tricks. If East plays *low,* waiting to capture dummy's king with his ace, the defenders take two tricks.

Of course, there are exceptions to second hand low. You may, for instance, be able to win a trick or prevent declarer from winning an undeserved trick at *no cost.* In the following examples, spades is trumps, and declarer is leading hearts.

$$\heartsuit \text{ Q 5}$$
$$\heartsuit \text{ K J 9 4 2} \quad \blacksquare$$

Declarer leads a low heart toward dummy. Unless you fear that partner has the singleton ace or unless you want partner on lead so badly that you are willing to risk ducking, you should win. You may lose your king if you do not take it now.

Another time to play high in second seat is when you hold a sequence. Then you play a card that tells partner about your holding.

$$\text{9 6 3}$$
$$\text{A 4 2} \quad \blacksquare \quad \text{J 10 8 7}$$
$$\text{K Q 5}$$

Declarer leads this suit from dummy. Play the jack, revealing your good intermediates. When partner wins one of declarer's high cards with his ace, he will know it is both safe and desirable to lead this suit right back.

The Fine Points:

1. PLAY SECOND HAND HIGH when you can *kill a suit* declarer is trying to set up with a combination finesse.

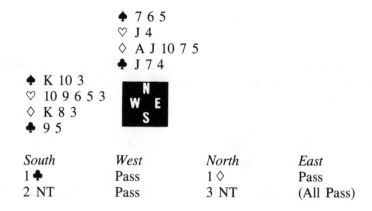

South	West	North	East
1 ♣	Pass	1 ◇	Pass
2 NT	Pass	3 NT	(All Pass)

28

You lead the ♡ 5. Partner covers dummy's jack with the king, and declarer wins the ace. **What do you do when declarer leads a diamond toward dummy?**

You must assume that declarer has a low doubleton diamond, since nothing you do will affect the outcome if he has Q-x, Q-x-x, or x-x-x. Insert your ◇ K, which may prevent declarer from using dummy's suit. It is true that, if you play low and declarer finesses dummy's 10 or jack, partner can duck with Q-x-x and shut the diamonds out. But declarer then takes two diamond tricks when he is entitled to only one. (You must hope, of course, that the ♣ J is not an entry to dummy.)

2. PLAY SECOND HAND HIGH when you need to win a trick *quickly* to return your partner's lead. We will see this type of play in the next chapter when we discuss defensive strategy vs. notrump and the importance of *preserving an entry* to the defenders' long suit. For now, here's an example at a *suit* contract.

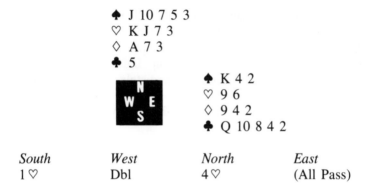

South	West	North	East
1 ♡	Dbl	4 ♡	(All Pass)

West leads the ◇ K, ducked by declarer. West shifts to a trump, and declarer draws two rounds, ending in dummy, as West discards a club. Next, declarer leads a low spade from dummy. **How do you defend?**

You should *hop up with your king*! If declarer has the ♠ A, you are not going to beat the contract. Declarer either has no spade losers or he will set up the spades and throw away his diamond losers. Judging by the play to the first trick and partner's refusal to continue diamonds, partner has K-Q-10-x. In that case, you must get in now and lead a diamond *through* declarer's jack, setting up a second diamond trick. The missing hands:

♠ A 9 6
♡ 4
◇ K Q 10 6
♣ K J 9 6 3

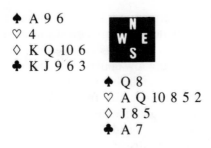

♠ Q 8
♡ A Q 10 8 5 2
◇ J 8 5
♣ A 7

Note the result if you fail to play the ♠K.

3. PLAY SECOND HAND HIGH when you can *block a suit* or *kill an entry* declarer needs.

```
            K 9 6 5 3 2
  J 8 4         ■          A 10
            Q 7
```

Declarer leads this suit from dummy. If East plays low, declarer can win and duck the next trick to the bare ace, establishing the suit. East does better to play the ace on the first round. The suit is established, but the high cards are tangled up. If dummy has only one entry that the defenders can dislodge immediately, declarer can't use the long cards.

4. PLAY SECOND HAND HIGH when you must keep partner from being *endplayed*.

♠ Q 9 5 2
♡ A 9 4
◇ 8 4 2
♣ Q 4 2

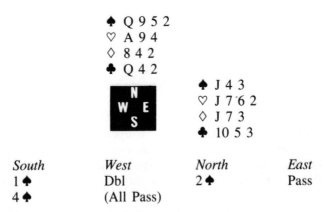

♠ J 4 3
♡ J 7 6 2
◇ J 7 3
♣ 10 5 3

South	West	North	East
1 ♠	Dbl	2 ♠	Pass
4 ♠	(All Pass)		

West leads the ♡K. Declarer ducks and wins the second heart lead. He ruffs a heart, draws three rounds of trumps, cashes the ♣A and ♣K and leads a club to the queen. Dummy then leads a low diamond. **How do you play to this trick?**

If you see what is coming, you'll be ready with the *jack*. If you lazily play low, declarer ducks the trick into your partner's hand, endplaying him. The diamond situation is:

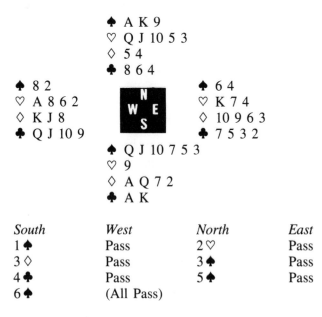

$\diamond$ 8 4 2

$\diamond$ A Q 10 5   ■ $\diamond$ J 7 3

$\diamond$ K 9 6

You need three diamond tricks to beat the contract, and if declarer's diamonds are Q-10-x or better, you can't get them. Be optimistic.

5. PLAY SECOND HAND HIGH when declarer is setting up a *ruffing finesse*.

$\spadesuit$ A K 9
$\heartsuit$ Q J 10 5 3
$\diamond$ 5 4
$\clubsuit$ 8 6 4

$\spadesuit$ 8 2 $\spadesuit$ 6 4
$\heartsuit$ A 8 6 2 $\heartsuit$ K 7 4
$\diamond$ K J 8 $\diamond$ 10 9 6 3
$\clubsuit$ Q J 10 9 $\clubsuit$ 7 5 3 2

$\spadesuit$ Q J 10 7 5 3
$\heartsuit$ 9
$\diamond$ A Q 7 2
$\clubsuit$ A K

South	*West*	*North*	*East*
1 $\spadesuit$	Pass	2 $\heartsuit$	Pass
3 $\diamond$	Pass	3 $\spadesuit$	Pass
4 $\clubsuit$	Pass	5 $\spadesuit$	Pass
6 $\spadesuit$	(All Pass)		

West leads the $\clubsuit$ Q against the slam. Hoping to avoid the diamond finesse, declarer goes to dummy with a trump and leads a low heart. East knows declarer does not have the singleton $\heartsuit$ A (declarer would cash it early), and if declarer has the A-9, the contract is probably unbeatable. So East puts up the $\heartsuit$ K, winning, and returns a trump. Declarer must lose another trick for down one.

Note what happens if East plays low. Declarer's 9 loses to the ace, but he can ruff out the $\heartsuit$ K later and return to dummy with a trump to cash the good hearts.

IIb. *COVERING HONORS*

An exception to the tendency toward second hand low may occur when declarer *leads an intermediate card.* Then you may gain by *covering* with an intermediate of your own. If you make declarer spend two high cards on the same trick, your lower cards may assume some stature. Here is a simple case:

```
           Q 5
9 8 4 3    ■          K 7 2
           A J 10 6
```

Declarer attacks this suit by leading dummy's queen. He will take four tricks if East ducks. But if East covers with the king, declarer must use his queen and ace on the same trick. West's 9 will control the fourth round.

Some positions aren't as obvious.

```
           10 4
Q 9 6 3    ■          A 5
           K J 8 7 2
```

Declarer attacks this suit by leading the 10 from dummy. East gains a trick by capturing the 10 with his ace. If East ducks, his ace will capture only low cards when declarer leads the 4 from dummy later.

Now let's see when you should *not* automatically cover an honor.
1. DON'T COVER if it's impossible to promote any tricks by covering. Remember the reason for covering an honor!

```
    ♠ J 6
    ■              ♠ Q 5 3
```

Spades is trumps, declarer having bid and rebid the suit. At some point he leads the ♠J from the table. You accomplish nothing by covering; play low as smoothly as you can. If you play low *without a giveaway pause,* declarer may refuse to finesse against you, playing your partner for the trump queen.
   DON'T COVER if you have a key honor that declarer can't capture.

A 7 5

K 6 3 2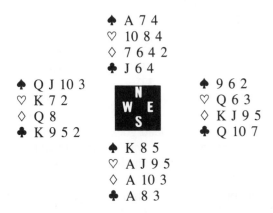

Suppose this suit is trumps. Declarer leads the queen from his hand. You should certainly *duck*, protecting your king. It wouldn't be as clear to duck if this were a side suit, since declarer could be trying to fool you by leading the unsupported queen (a play known as a *Chinese finesse)*.

DON'T COVER if declarer may be taking a combination finesse that he lacks the entries to complete.

```
                      ♠ A 7 4
                      ♡ 10 8 4
                      ◇ 7 6 4 2
                      ♣ J 6 4
      ♠ Q J 10 3            N          ♠ 9 6 2
      ♡ K 7 2          W         E     ♡ Q 6 3
      ◇ Q 8                 S          ◇ K J 9 5
      ♣ K 9 5 2                        ♣ Q 10 7
                      ♠ K 8 5
                      ♡ A J 9 5
                      ◇ A 10 3
                      ♣ A 8 3
```

South played at 1 NT. He won the ♠ Q opening lead in dummy and led the ♡ 10, tempting East to cover. East, however, could see that the lead would never be in dummy again, so he withheld his queen. Declarer lost to the ♡ K and had to concede a trick to East's queen later.

DON'T COVER when declarer has options, and a cover will solve his problems.

```
               ♠ 6 5 3
               ♡ A K 10 3
               ◇ Q 10 4
               ♣ J 10 8
  ♠ K J 9 4 2      N        ♠ Q 10 7
  ♡ Q 7 6        W   E      ♡ 9 8 4 2
  ◇ K 8           S         ◇ 7 5 3
  ♣ 7 4 3                   ♣ 9 6 2
               ♠ A 8
               ♡ J 5
               ◇ A J 9 6 2
               ♣ A K Q 5
```

South	West	North	East
1 ◇	Pass	1 ♡	Pass
3 ♣	Pass	3 ◇	Pass
3 NT	Pass	Pass	Pass

You are West. When your spade lead goes to the queen and ace,
you know almost the entire deal. Since South must hold all the missing high cards to justify his jump shift, he has eight top tricks (one
spade, two hearts, one diamond, four clubs). When declarer leads
the ♡J, you duck smoothly. Now declarer must guess which red-
suit finesse to take to make his contract.

It is seldom right to cover when dummy leads an honor from a
strong holding such as Q-J-10-9-x. How should you play when dummy
has a *broken* sequence?

This example shows the textbook rule:

```
            J 10 3
  K 9 5     ■        Q 7 6
            A 8 4 2
```

Declarer leads the jack from dummy. If East covers, declarer wins
his ace and returns a low card toward dummy. West cannot prevent
declarer from bringing in the suit with only one loser. East should
duck the jack but cover if the 10, the *last* equal in the broken sequence, is led later. The defenders will take two tricks.

There are, alas, a couple of exceptions to the idea of covering the
last of touching honors. If you hold an honor that is not well guard-
ed, you may do best to go ahead and cover early.

```
            J 10 8
              ■              K 9 (or Q 9)
```

If declarer leads the jack, cover (unless you think declarer has a *seven*-card suit). If declarer has A-x-x-x-x, A-Q-x-x-x or K-x-x-x-x-x, you offer him the option of finessing with dummy's 8 later. You give the show away if you follow with the 9.

Another problem in covering honors in a broken sequence occurs when you have more than one honor.

```
              10 9 3
  8 7 6         ■             K J 4
              A Q 5 2
```

Declarer leads the 10 from dummy. East must cover (and cover again if dummy leads the 9 later).

IIIa. *THIRD-HAND PLAY*

The Basics:

The tendency in third seat is exactly *opposite* that of second seat. Third to play, you often put up a *high* card. The basis for this tendency is the same as the basis for covering honors: the prospect of promoting intermediate cards. By playing a high card in third seat, you make declarer pay a price to win the trick and may promote lower cards in partner's hand (or in your own hand).

The general idea is seen here:

```
               ♡ 8 4 2
  ♡ Q 10 6 3     ■            ♡ K 9 5
               ♡ A J 7
```

West leads the ♡3, and East must play the *king* in third seat. Declarer wins the ace, but West's intermediates are promoted. The defenders will take two tricks if East can get in to lead through declarer's jack. If East plays a cowardly *9* on partner's lead, declarer wins an undeserved trick with the jack and also scores his ace.

Third hand high has many exceptions. Remember the basic idea. If sacrificing a high card in third seat has nothing to gain, do not feel obliged to play it.

♠ Q J 10 9
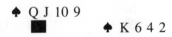
♠ K 6 4 2

Hearts is trumps, and partner's opening lead is the ♠ 3. Do not play the king. Declarer has the ♠ A, since partner wouldn't underlead an ace against a heart contract. You will only establish winners for declarer if you play high in third seat this time. Maybe declarer has the *singleton* ace and must play his ace regardless.

♠ Q 7 4

♠ K 10 2

Hearts is still trumps, and your partner leads the ♠3 again. Declarer plays low from dummy. Once more, you know declarer has the ♠ A, so the king can't be the right play. *Finesse your 10,* hoping partner led from the jack, and the 10 will force out declarer's ace. If your holding were K-9-2, you would play the 9. So long as you know declarer has the ace, withhold your king.

♠ A 10 5
■
♠ J 8 4

Your partner leads the 2, and declarer plays low from dummy. Partner would have led the king with both the king and queen, so declarer surely has an honor. Therefore, play the *8,* saving a trick if the situation is:

♠ A 10 5
♠ Q 9 6 2 ■ ♠ J 8 4
♠ K 7 3

If you are third hand to play from a *sequence*, play the *lowest* card in the sequence. As usual, the idea is to let partner in on what you have.

7 6 5
K 8 4 2 ■ Q J 10
A 9 3

West leads the 2. East, with a sequence to play from in third seat, puts up his *10.* When the 10 forces declarer's ace, West can infer that his partner has the jack and queen also. Declarer wouldn't spend his ace to win the trick (setting up a defender's king) if he could win cheaply. If East plays the *queen* and declarer wins, West can't tell where the other honors lie.

Note that third hand's play from equals is just the opposite of leading from equals. This is another standard practice that makes defending easier.

$$\diamond \; 8\,6\,4$$

$\diamond$ K 9 7 5 3 2   ■

You lead the $\diamond$ 5 against a notrump contract. Dummy plays low, partner contributes the jack, declarer wins the queen. **Who has the** *ace*? Clearly, declarer has the ace — your partner would have played the ace if had it. **Who has the 10?** Declarer has the 10. If partner had the jack and 10, he would have played the lower of his equals. So you know declarer holds A-Q-10. If you lead this suit again, you'll give away a trick.

The Fine Points:
1. With A-Q-x (rarely, A-J-x) in partner's suit, be ready to *finesse in third seat to keep communication with partner and stop a holdup play by declarer.*

♠ 9 5

♠ J 8 7 4 2   ■   ♠ A Q 6

♠ K 10 3

Defending against notrump, West leads the ♠4. If East wins the ace and returns the queen, declarer *holds up* the king, possibly isolating West's long cards. But suppose East plays the queen at the first trick. Declarer must win immediately, since, for all he knows, West has led from A-J-x-x-x! The defenders' suit is now set up, and the lines of communication are open. (Note that playing the ♠Q cannot cost; if West has the king, the queen is as good a card as the ace.)

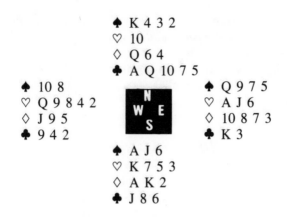

♠ K 4 3 2
♥ 10
⋄ Q 6 4
♣ A Q 10 7 5

♠ 10 8
♥ Q 9 8 4 2
⋄ J 9 5
♣ 9 4 2

♠ Q 9 7 5
♥ A J 6
⋄ 10 8 7 3
♣ K 3

♠ A J 6
♥ K 7 5 3
⋄ A K 2
♣ J 8 6

South is declarer at 3 NT, and West leads the ♡4. East must play his jack to preserve communication and defeat the contract. (This is not an impossible play; East knows that West is more likely to have the ♡Q than the king, since he can have very few high-card points on the bidding.)

2. Third hand may have a chance for a *discovery* play.

♡ 7 5 3
   ♡ K J 2

West leads the ♡4 against 4♠. **Who has the ♡A?** You know declarer has the ♡A, so you can play your ♡J in third seat, *discovering who has the* ♡Q. If declarer wins the queen, you may judge to switch suits if you gain the lead.

3. A *deep* finesse by third hand may be worth considering.

♠ J 8
   ♠ A 9 4

Partner leads the ♠2 against notrump, and dummy plays the 8. With declarer known to have four cards to at least one honor (partner would not lead low from K-Q-10-x), your best play may be the 9. The layout could be.

♠ J 8
♠ K 7 5 2   ■   ♠ A 9 4
♠ Q 10 6 3

Your side will take three tricks instead of two. Note that you would play the *ace* against a suit contract.

Look at this position again:

♠ J 8 6
■   ♠ K 9 4

West leads the ♠ 5 against a 4 ♡ contract, and dummy plays low. We suggested you *withhold the king*, since declarer is marked with the ace. Actually, assuming the 5 is partner's fourth-highest spade, you can be *sure* your 9 will force the ace. Partner has three spades higher than the 5. They must be the queen, 10 and 7, since those are the only spades not in view! This leads us to . . .

IIIb. *THE RULE OF ELEVEN*

Instead of working out partner's holding as you did in the example above, you can apply the *Rule of Eleven*. This is a device the defenders can use to judge the play, especially third-hand play.

> IF PARTNER LEADS THE FOURTH-HIGHEST CARD IN HIS SUIT, SUBTRACT THE SPOT FROM 11. THE REMAINDER IS THE NUMBER OF HIGHER-RANKING CARDS THAT LIE IN THE OTHER THREE HANDS.

Apply the rule in the situation above:

♠ J 8 6
♠ 5 led   ■   ♠ K 9 4

Subtract five, partner's spot, from 11. The remainder is six. So your hand, declarer's hand and dummy contain six cards higher than partner's 5. You can see five of them: the 6, 7, 9, J and K. So declarer has only one card higher than partner's 5 (and it must be the ace).

♠ Q 9 4 2

■   ♠ K J 6

West leads the ♠5 (which we will assume is fourth-highest) against 4♡. Dummy plays low. **What should East play?** Subtract five, partner's spot, from 11. The remainder is six. There are six cards about the table higher than partner's 5. You can see five of them, so declarer has only *one* card higher than the 5 — and again it must be the ace. East's correct play is the 6.

Let's apply the Rule of Eleven in a full deal:

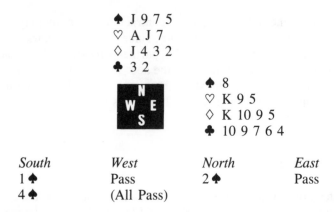

♠ J 9 7 5
♡ A J 7
◇ J 4 3 2
♣ 3 2

♠ 8
♡ K 9 5
◇ K 10 9 5
♣ 10 9 7 6 4

South	West	North	East
1♠	Pass	2♠	Pass
4♠	(All Pass)		

West leads the ♡6, and declarer plays low from dummy. **How do you defend?**

Apply the Rule of Eleven. Six from 11 leaves five — five cards around the table higher than partner's 6. Since you can see all five, you can win with the 9. It would be fatal to play the king, since the missing cards are:

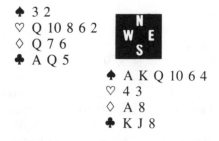

♠ 3 2
♡ Q 10 8 6 2
◇ Q 7 6
♣ A Q 5

♠ A K Q 10 6 4
♡ 4 3
◇ A 8
♣ K J 8

If East plays his king at trick one, declarer can finesse dummy's jack later to get a discard for his diamond loser.

40

You can use the Rule of Eleven *when your partner returns your lead.* You need only be sure that his card is his original fourth highest.

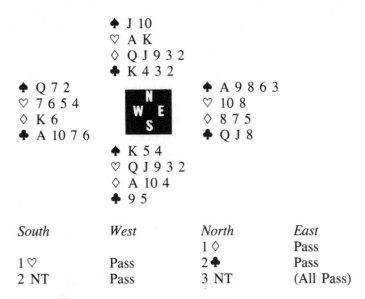

```
                    ♠ J 10
                    ♡ A K
                    ◊ Q J 9 3 2
                    ♣ K 4 3 2
  ♠ Q 7 2                         ♠ A 9 8 6 3
  ♡ 7 6 5 4          N            ♡ 10 8
  ◊ K 6          W       E        ◊ 8 7 5
  ♣ A 10 7 6         S            ♣ Q J 8
                    ♠ K 5 4
                    ♡ Q J 9 3 2
                    ◊ A 10 4
                    ♣ 9 5
```

South	West	North	East
		1 ◊	Pass
1 ♡	Pass	2 ♣	Pass
2 NT	Pass	3 NT	(All Pass)

West leads the ♠2 (choosing the unbid suit). East wins the ace and returns the 6, his original fourth highest. Since declarer suspects that the spades are divided 4-4 and he fears a club shift anyway, he wins the second trick. West must be careful. If East's ♠6 is his original fourth-highest spade, the Rule of Eleven applies. Six from 11 leaves five, meaning that five cards higher than the 6 lie in West's hand, declarer's hand and dummy. West has seen all five. Since declarer has nothing higher than the 6 left, West can unblock his ♠Q under the king safely. When West wins the ◊K, the defenders will take all the spades.

To review:

The defenders must often rely on general principles for guidance as they play routinely to each trick (especially in the early play).

1. Once you decide what suit to lead, the card you choose is often predetermined. For instance, with a sequence (three or more cards adjacent in rank, of which the highest card is an honor) lead the top card in the sequence.

2. The tendency in second-hand play is to wait by playing a low card. You don't need desperate tactics when your partner will get to play last. This tendency has many exceptions.

3. The most important exception to *second hand low* may occur when declarer leads an intermediate card. Then you may want to cover with an intermediate of your own. By forcing declarer to spend two high cards on the same trick, you may promote lower cards.

4. The tendency by third hand is to play high. Again, you may promote intermediate cards. *Third hand high* has many exceptions — if you cannot gain by sacrificing a high card in third position, you aren't obligated to play it. As third hand to play from a sequence, play the lowest card.

5. The Rule of Eleven is a device the defenders use to make judgments in third-hand play.

I. QUIZ ON CHOOSING A CARD TO LEAD

1. The opponents reach 4♠. Your side did not bid. You decide to lead a heart. Choose the proper card from these holdings.

1.	♡ K Q J 5	9.	♡ A J 8 6 4
2.	♡ Q J 9 6 3	10.	♡ J 10 5
3.	♡ Q 10 8 6 4	11.	♡ 8 4 2
4.	♡ K Q 4 2	12.	♡ A K 7 5 3
5.	♡ Q J 7	13.	♡ A K
6.	♡ K 10 9 8 4	14.	♡ 10 9 8 5 3
7.	♡ 9 8 7 4 2	15.	♡ Q 9 8 7 4
8.	♡ A J 8 6 4	16.	♡ K Q

2. The opponents reach 3 NT. Your side did not bid. You decide to lead a diamond. Choose the proper card from these holdings.

1.	◊ K Q J 5 4	6.	◊ J 9 7 2
2.	◊ Q J 9 7 6	7.	◊ A J 8 5 3
3.	◊ Q J 6 5 4	8.	◊ 9 8 7 5 3
4.	◊ J 9 7 6 4 2	9.	◊ 10 9 8 7 4
5.	◊ A J 10 8 5	10.	◊ K 9 8 7 4

II. QUIZ ON SECOND-HAND PLAY

1. Dummy has ♠942. At some point, declarer leads a low spade from dummy. Choose the correct play from these holdings.

1.	♠ K J 6 3	4.	♠ A K 7 5 3
2.	♠ A 7 5	5.	♠ Q J 5
3.	♠ K Q J 7	6.	♠ K Q 6 5

2. Dummy leads low from K-7-5. You are to play in second seat from A-J-4. Which card is usually correct?

3. Dummy leads low from K-7-5. You are to play next with Q-J-6. Which card do you play?

4. Declarer is playing a heart contract and leads a spade from his hand toward dummy's Q-5. You are next to play from K-J-9-7. Which card do you play?

III. QUIZ ON COVERING HONORS

In these situations, decide whether you would *cover* the honor led by declarer.

1. Q 6
    ■   K 9 8 5   Dummy leads the queen at notrump.

2. J 7
    ■   Q 4   Dummy leads the jack at notrump.

3.   A K J 7 6   Declarer leads the 10 at notrump.
    Q 8   ■

4.   A 10 9 8   Declarer leads the jack at notrump.
    Q 6 5   ■

5. Q 6
    ■   K 5 4 3   This suit is trumps. Declarer leads the queen from dummy.

6. J 10 4
    ■   Q 7 6   Dummy leads the jack at notrump.

7.   ♠ 7 6 3
           ♡ A 7 3
           ◊ A 10 4
           ♣ Q 9 6 3

    ♠ Q 10 8 4 2
    ♡ J 9 2   N
    ◊ Q 5 2   W   E
    ♣ K 4   S

South opened 1 NT, North raised to 3 NT. You lead the ♠4 to partner's jack and declarer's king. At trick two declarer leads the ◊J. Do you cover?

IV. QUIZ ON THIRD-HAND PLAY

In these situations, declarer is playing 4 ♠, and your partner leads the ♡2. When dummy plays low, what do you play in third seat?

1. ♡ 7 6 4
    ■   ♡ K 9 5

2. ♡ Q 6 5
    ■   ♡ K 10 4 3

3. ♡ A 10 7
    ■   ♡ Q 9 6 4

4. ♡ 7 6 5
    ■   ♡ J 10 9

5. ♡ 7 6 5
    ■   ♡ K Q 8 4

6. ♡ J 8 6
    ■   ♡ K 10 9 5

7. ♡ 8 6 4
    ■   ♡ A J 7

8. You led the ◊4 from K-10-8-4-3 against a 3 NT contract. Dummy has 9-2 and plays low. Your partner plays the queen, and declarer wins the ace. Who has the ◊J?

QUIZ ON THE RULE OF ELEVEN

1.   ♠ Q 9 4 3
    ■   ♠ K J 6

West leads the ♠5 against a 4♡ contract. Dummy plays low. Which spade do you play?

2.

♠ Q 8 6 4
♡ Q 8 6 4
◊ A J 7
♣ 6 5

♠ 7 5
♡ K J 7
◊ K 9 3
♣ J 8 7 4 3

South opened 1♠, North raised to 2♠, South jumped to 4♠. West leads the ◊6, and dummy plays the 7. What do you play as East?

SOLUTIONS TO QUIZ ON CHOOSING A CARD TO LEAD

1. 1. K   9. A
    2. Q   10. J
    3. 6   11. 8
    4. K (to assure *one* trick)   12. A
    5. Q (from three cards, lead   13. K (from A-K *alone*)
       the queen even though   14. 10
       you don't have a true   15. 7
       sequence)   16. K
    6. 10
    7. 9
    8. A
2. 1. K   6. 2
    2. Q   7. 5
    3. 5   8. 9
    4. 6   9. 10
    5. J   10. 7

SOLUTIONS TO QUIZ ON SECOND-HAND PLAY

1.   1. 3
   2. 5
   3. K,   suggesting a sequence.
   4. K,   but it could be right to duck, giving declarer a guess if he has Q-10-x.
   5. 5
   6. 5,   unless you need to assure *one* trick, in which case play the king.
2. Play the *4.* Perhaps you will take tricks with both your ace *and* jack.
3. Play the *queen,* to assure one trick.
4. Play the king to win the trick. To win cannot cost, and you may never get your king if you don't take it now.

SOLUTIONS TO QUIZ ON COVERING HONORS

1. Cover, with your good intermediate cards. You can assure at least one trick.
2. Cover.
3. Cover. Perhaps partner has 9-x-x-x.
4. Don't cover. Dummy has all the intermediates, so to cover gains nothing.
5. Don't cover. Protect your king as a sure trick.
6. Don't cover, but cover if dummy leads the 10 later.
7. Don't cover. Declarer is probably trying to set up his best suit, so you will probably help *him* if you cover.

SOLUTIONS TO QUIZ ON THIRD-HAND PLAY

1. K   5. Q
2. 10   6. 9
3. 9   7. A
4. 9   8. Declarer. Partner would play the jack in third seat from Q-J.

SOLUTIONS TO QUIZ ON THE RULE OF ELEVEN

1. Play the 6. The Rule of Eleven tells you that declarer has only one spade higher than partner's 5, and it must be the ace.
2. Play the ◊ 9. Declarer has no diamonds higher than partner's 6.

QUIZ ON ADVANCED IDEAS IN DEFENSIVE PLAY

1.
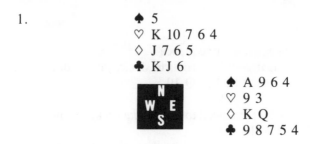
```
        ♠ 5
        ♡ K 10 7 6 4
        ◊ J 7 6 5
        ♣ K J 6
                        ♠ A 9 6 4
                        ♡ 9 3
                        ◊ K Q
                        ♣ 9 8 7 5 4
```

South opened 1 ♡, North raised to 4 ♡. West leads the ♠ J, and you win the ace. What do you lead at trick two?

2.
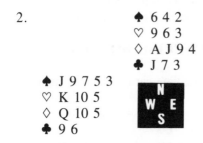
```
                ♠ 6 4 2
                ♡ 9 6 3
                ◊ A J 9 4
                ♣ J 7 3
    ♠ J 9 7 5 3
    ♡ K 10 5
    ◊ Q 10 5
    ♣ 9 6
```

South opened 1 ♣, North responded 1 ◊, South jumped to 3 NT. Your spade lead goes to the 6, queen and king. Declarer then leads a low diamond toward dummy. Plan your defense.

3.

```
        ♠ 7 6
        ♡ A 6 5
        ◊ K Q 10 5 4
        ♣ Q 8 7
                        ♠ A Q 5
                        ♡ 9 8 7 4
                        ◊ A 3 2
                        ♣ J 9 3
```

South opened 1 NT, North raised to 3 NT. West leads the ♠ 4. Plan your defense.

4.

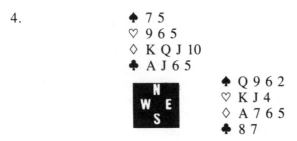

♠ 7 5
♡ 9 6 5
◇ K Q J 10
♣ A J 6 5

♠ Q 9 6 2
♡ K J 4
◇ A 7 6 5
♣ 8 7

South opened 1♣, North responded 1◇; South rebid 2♣, North raised to 3♣; South jumped to 5♣. West leads the ♡2. Plan your defense.

5.

♠ 9 4
♡ A 6 5
◇ K 7 6 5
♣ K 7 6 5

♠ Q J 3
♡ Q 9 8 4 2
◇ Q 4 3 2
♣ 4

South opened 1 NT, North raised to 3 NT. West leads the ♠7. Your jack is won by declarer's king. Declarer leads a club to dummy's king and a club back toward his hand. What do you discard on this trick?

6.

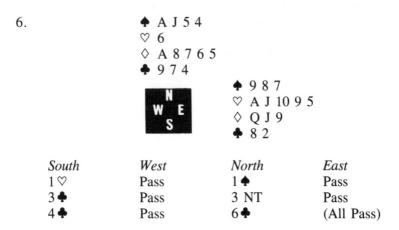

♠ A J 5 4
♡ 6
◇ A 8 7 6 5
♣ 9 7 4

♠ 9 8 7
♡ A J 10 9 5
◇ Q J 9
♣ 8 2

South	West	North	East
1 ♡	Pass	1 ♠	Pass
3 ♣	Pass	3 NT	Pass
4 ♣	Pass	6 ♣	(All Pass)

West leads the ♠K. Dummy wins the ace and leads a low heart. Plan your defense.

SOLUTIONS

1. Shift to the ◇ Q. You must cash what diamond tricks you can. (If declarer holds the ◇ A, you probably can't set him.) But if you lead the normal ◇ K and follow with the queen, partner will play low with A-x-x-x, waiting for a third round. He should grasp the significance of your unusual diamond plays, overtake the king and give you a ruff.

2. Play the ◇ Q, gaining a trick if declarer holds two or three low cards. You have nothing to lose by making this play — if declarer holds the ◇ K, he is about to finesse dummy's jack successfully.

3. Play the ♠ Q, forcing declarer to win if he has K-x-x and keeping communication with your partner's hand. You'll lead the ♠ A and another spade when you win the ◇ A, hoping partner started with J-x-x-x-x. If you win the ♠ A at trick one, declarer can hold up his king effectively.

4. Play the ♡ J as a *discovery* play. If declarer wins the ♡ Q, you'll give up on hearts and switch to spades when you win the ◇ A.

5. Discard the ♠ Q. The Rule of Eleven indicates that the king was declarer's only spade higher than partner's 7, so all of partner's spades are now good. However, partner cannot know that — from his vantage point, declarer may have the ♠ Q. You must discard the queen so partner will know he can cash his spades if he gets in (possibly with a club trick).

6. You should *duck* the heart lead. You won't lose your ace, since declarer can't ruff *all* his hearts in dummy. If declarer's hearts are K-Q-x-x-x, you gain by letting him win only *one* honor. If you put up your ace, he scores both the king and queen. One trick could be crucial on this deal.

Chapter 3

STRATEGY vs. NOTRUMP

You have learned some principles to remember as you play routinely to a trick. You also saw that you sometimes must think for yourself and depart from those principles.

When we discussed leads, you learned that, once you decide what *suit* to lead, the *card* you pick is often a routine matter. But choosing a suit requires more judgment. How do you approach the defense? What suits should you lead to get the tricks you need?

You have three possible approaches to the defense at notrump:

I.   ACTIVE. The most common strategy is the attempt to establish *long* cards. Setting up a long suit is usually your best hope of tricks when declarer's side has most of the *high* cards. With the opening lead as an advantage, the defense plugs away at its longest suit at every opportunity, racing to set up long cards before declarer has the tricks he needs. Without a compelling reason to switch, the defenders will stick relentlessly to the suit they start with.

One implicit problem in this approach: Even if the defense sets up long cards, the player that has them must get the lead. Therefore, the defenders must take care to preserve an *entry* in the hand where the winners lie or will lie. This idea may affect the choice of opening leads against notrump. For example, if you hold:

♠ A 5 2
♡ 6 5 2
◇ K 10 8 5 3
♣ A 3

and you hear the opponents bid 1 NT-3 NT, you routinely lead your ◇ 5. But with:

♠ 6 4 2
♡ J 10
◇ J 8 6 4 2
♣ 7 4 2

a diamond lead is less attractive. Even if can set up your suit, you have no way to gain the lead to cash the winners. Sometimes you should try to establish your *partner's* long suit, and the ♡ J opening lead would be the choice of many players.

This deal shows how the defenders must worry about communication in notrump defense.

1.
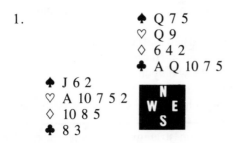

　　　　　　　　　♠ Q 7 5
　　　　　　　　　♡ Q 9
　　　　　　　　　◇ 6 4 2
　　　　　　　　　♣ A Q 10 7 5
♠ J 6 2
♡ A 10 7 5 2
◇ 10 8 5
♣ 8 3

South opened 1 NT, and North raised to 3 NT. West leads the ♡ 5. Declarer plays low from dummy, and East produces the king, winning the trick. Declarer follows low to the first heart. East returns the ♡ 8, and declarer plays low again. **What should West do?**

Should West win the ace and return a third heart? He can establish his suit but without an entry he can never cash the long hearts. Knowing that declarer has the ♡ J and is always entitled to one heart trick,

West should *duck* the second heart, allowing dummy's queen to win. If East wins a trick later, he can return a heart if he has one left, and *then* West wins and takes his long cards. To defeat the contract, West must save his entry until his suit is set up. The defenders, who have few high cards for entries, often use these ducking plays.

Suppose your *partner* is opening leader and has the long suit you must establish. Your objective should be to win an *early* trick and return your partner's lead. You must spend your entry early so you can set up his suit while he still has (you hope) an entry. Here's an illustrative deal.

2.

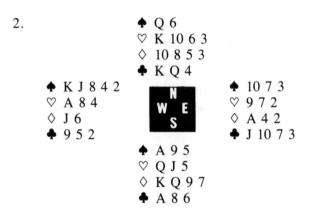

```
                    ♠ Q 6
                    ♡ K 10 6 3
                    ◊ 10 8 5 3
                    ♣ K Q 4
   ♠ K J 8 4 2                      ♠ 10 7 3
   ♡ A 8 4          N               ♡ 9 7 2
   ◊ J 6         W     E            ◊ A 4 2
   ♣ 9 5 2          S               ♣ J 10 7 3
                    ♠ A 9 5
                    ♡ Q J 5
                    ◊ K Q 9 7
                    ♣ A 8 6
```

You are East, defending 3 NT. West leads the ♠4. Declarer puts up dummy's queen, winning, and leads a low diamond from dummy at trick two. **What must East do to beat the contract?** East must go right up with his ace. This is no time to play second hand low. East uses his entry early so he can return a spade, establishing the suit while West still has the ♡A as an entry.

What happens if East plays low and declarer scores one quick diamond trick? With one trick in the bag, declarer shifts to hearts and sets up enough tricks in that suit to make 3 NT. *This type of play by East is common. It involves a basic idea in notrump defense.*

Look at this deal.

3.

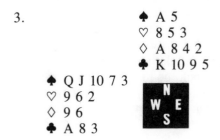

♠ A 5
♥ 8 5 3
♦ A 8 4 2
♣ K 10 9 5

♠ Q J 10 7 3
♥ 9 6 2
♦ 9 6
♣ A 8 3

You are defending 3 NT. South opened 1 NT, and North raised.
You lead your ♣ Q, of course. Declarer wins the ♠ A in dummy
and — get ready! — leads a club to his queen. **What do you do?**
If you recall the idea of clinging to your entry until your suit is set
up, you will *duck* at once. Perhaps declarer's clubs are Q-x-x-(x).
Then he will probably lead a second club (you duck again) and finesse
dummy's 10! Partner wins and sets up the spades while you still have
the ♣ A. Of course, if declarer has the ♣ J, your play won't help;
but if he lacks the jack, you must try to fool him.

Note that you must duck *smoothly*. If you hesitate before playing
low, declarer will know what is going on. Remember, *hang on to
your entry until your long suit is established.*

On rare occasions the defense may swap horses in the middle of
the deal. Perhaps the first suit they led looks hopeless, and time may
remain to establish another suit.

4.

♠ A Q J
♥ 7 5
♦ K 6 4
♣ J 10 8 6 4

♠ K 9
♥ Q J 10 8 4
♦ A 8 5 3
♣ 9 3

You are defending 3 NT. South opened 1 NT, and North raised
to game. West leads the ♠ 5. Declarer plays dummy's queen, and
you win the king. **Should you automatically return partner's lead
or look elsewhere for tricks?** If you are a realist, you will shift to
hearts. A spade return can't work. Since West is known to have at
most 3 high-card points on the bidding, he cannot have *two* entries,

which he needs to lead spades a third time to set up the suit, then get in to cash his winners. Perhaps, though, you can establish *your* suit and cash it. The other hands are:

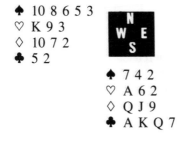

♠ 10 8 6 5 3
♡ K 9 3
◇ 10 7 2
♣ 5 2

♠ 7 4 2
♡ A 6 2
◇ Q J 9
♣ A K Q 7

After a heart shift, declarer has only eight tricks and must lead a diamond sooner or later, letting you cash your winners. Returning your partner's lead is not an inviolable rule. (Declarer can assure the contract by playing the ♠A at trick one and knocking out the ◇A. That would be the correct play at rubber bridge. At match-point duplicate, declarer must finesse in spades, risking his contract, because overtricks are so likely.)

II. PASSIVE. If dummy is weak in high cards and lacks a long suit, declarer may have a hard time establishing tricks. *If the contract seems to be touch-and-go,* an active approach may lose. By leading from your honors in an attempt to set up long cards, you may give away crucial tricks. In a PASSIVE approach you try to *exit safely* whenever you must lead. Declarer may come up short of tricks, especially if you don't help him.

A passive strategy may be clear when you choose your opening lead. Look at this situation.

North	South
	1 ♣
1 ♠	1 NT
2 NT	Pass

55

As West, what do you lead from:

5. ♠ 8 3
    ♡ K 7 6 2
    ◇ J 9 5
    ♣ K 10 9 6

A case exists for a safe, passive defense. You can start by leading a spade through dummy's suit. Perhaps this is not dynamic, but it is fairly safe. Imagine how the play will go. First, the opponents have *no extra strength,* so declarer may have trouble scraping up eight tricks. He may have unpleasant guesses in choosing which suits to lead and how to attack them. Also, your black-suit holdings suggest that declarer won't take many tricks in those suits; you have the clubs sewed up, and partner surely has at least four spades. A spade lead is unlikely to set up tricks, but *you may not need to establish long cards to prevail* . The contract may die of natural causes when declarer runs out of tricks. A heart lead may let you set up a long heart eventually, but it may give away a crucial trick in the process.

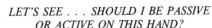

LET'S SEE . . . SHOULD I BE PASSIVE OR ACTIVE ON THIS HAND?

6.

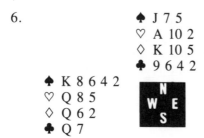

♠ J 7 5
♡ A 10 2
◇ K 10 5
♣ 9 6 4 2

♠ K 8 6 4 2
♡ Q 8 5
◇ Q 6 2
♣ Q 7

You are defending 3 NT. South opened 1 NT, North raised to 2 NT and South went on to game. Your spade lead is covered by the 5, 9 and queen. Declarer then leads a heart to the ace and a heart back to his jack. You win the queen. **What do you do?** Since dummy is weakish and lacks a long suit, go passive. Get out with your last heart and let declarer struggle with his anemic dummy. If you lead anything but a heart, you may give away a trick — possibly the ninth trick!

III. KILLING A SUIT. Sometimes it will be obvious that the contract will fail if the defenders prevent declarer from using his long suit. In this case, the focus shifts to an attack on declarer's *communication.* The defense must forget about setting up a suit of their own. If they can keep declarer from winning long-card tricks, he is bound to run out of high-card tricks eventually.

7.

♠ K J
♡ 7
◇ 9 7 5 2
♣ Q 10 8 6 4 3

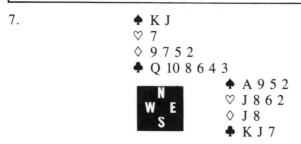

♠ A 9 5 2
♡ J 8 6 2
◇ J 8
♣ K J 7

You defend 3 NT. Partner leads the ♡3, and declarer wins your jack with the queen. He cashes the ♣A, partner following low, and continues with a low club. Partner discards, and declarer plays dummy's 10, losing to your jack. **What do you lead?** Should you return your partner's lead or switch priorities? The hearts can wait, especially since partner has only four. Return a low spade, killing declarer's obvious entry to the club suit. Without club tricks, declarer will surely fail. (It's better to lead a low spade than the ace, then a low spade; save the ♠ A to get in for a heart return.)

The defense can also cause trouble by *holding up a winner* and ruining declarer's communication. In this deal a defender held up with *two* winners in a suit.

8.

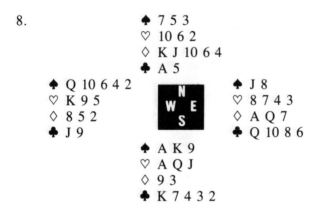

	♠ 7 5 3	
	♡ 10 6 2	
	◇ K J 10 6 4	
	♣ A 5	
♠ Q 10 6 4 2		♠ J 8
♡ K 9 5		♡ 8 7 4 3
◇ 8 5 2		◇ A Q 7
♣ J 9		♣ Q 10 8 6
	♠ A K 9	
	♡ A Q J	
	◇ 9 3	
	♣ K 7 4 3 2	

South opens 1 NT, North raises to 2 NT and South goes on to game. The opening lead is the ♣4. Declarer ducks East's jack, damaging the defenders' communication in *their* suit, and wins the spade return. Next, he passes the ◇9. **What should East do?**

East should *duck* the first diamond and win the second. Declarer, out of diamonds, lacks the communication to set up the diamonds and return to dummy to cash them. Note the difference if East wins the *first* diamond.

Don't forget the possibility of KILLING A SUIT in *declarer's* hand.

9.

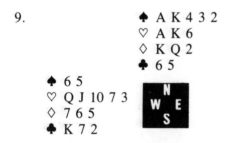

	♠ A K 4 3 2
	♡ A K 6
	◇ K Q 2
	♣ 6 5
♠ 6 5	
♡ Q J 10 7 3	
◇ 7 6 5	
♣ K 7 2	

You are defending 3 NT. North opened 1 ♠ and raised South's 1 NT response to game. Declarer ducks your ♡ Q opening and wins the continuation. He then leads a club from dummy and plays the 10 from his hand. If declarer's hand is:

♠ 7		♠ 7
♡ 8 5 2		♡ 8 5 2
◇ J 9 3	or	◇ A 9 3
♣ A Q 10 9 4 3		♣ Q J 10 9 4 3

you must refuse this trick; otherwise, declarer will bring in the clubs and make his game.

The next deal is a holdover from the chapter on basic ideas, but the situation bears repeating.

10.
                    ♠ A 5
                    ♡ J 8 3
                    ◇ 7 4
                    ♣ A J 10 7 5 2
    ♠ J 9 7 4 2
    ♡ K 10 4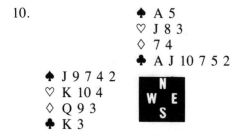
    ◇ Q 9 3
    ♣ K 3

You defend 3 NT. South opened 1 ◇, North responded 2 ♣, South rebid 2 NT (showing a balanced minimum) and North raised to 3 NT. Declarer ducks your spade opening lead in dummy. East produces the king and returns a spade to the ace, declarer following low. Declarer then leads a diamond to his ace and a club toward dummy. To kill a suit, you must put up your *king*. If declarer has two low clubs (the critical holding), you can stop him from ducking the first club to your partner and cut his link with dummy. (If West plays low, East can *duck* dummy's 10 or jack with his Q-x-x and shut out the clubs. But then declarer gets two club tricks when he deserves only one. If his hand is:

                    ♠ Q 10 x
                    ♡ A x x
                    ◇ A K x x x
                    ♣ x x

he can concede a diamond and finish with nine tricks.)

Let's review the possible strategies against notrump:

I.	*ACTIVE:*	The defenders plug away at a long suit, hoping to establish it. They must take care to *preserve an entry* to the long cards.
II.	*PASSIVE:*	The defenders try to *lead safely* and avoid giving declarer undeserved tricks. Declarer may fall short of his contract without high cards and good suits to develop. In this approach, the defenders may lead from a sequential holding, lead back a suit declarer has led first or lead a suit in which declarer clearly has strength.
III.	*KILLING A SUIT:*	The defenders try to deny declarer his best source of tricks. They attack declarer's communication by forcing out his entries prematurely and holding up their high cards.

Our last deal illustrates some of these techniques:

11.

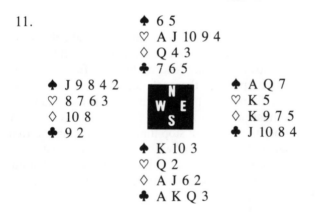

```
                    ♠ 6 5
                    ♡ A J 10 9 4
                    ◇ Q 4 3
                    ♣ 7 6 5
     ♠ J 9 8 4 2              ♠ A Q 7
     ♡ 8 7 6 3     N          ♡ K 5
     ◇ 10 8      W   E        ◇ K 9 7 5
     ♣ 9 2         S          ♣ J 10 8 4
                    ♠ K 10 3
                    ♡ Q 2
                    ◇ A J 6 2
                    ♣ A K Q 3
```

South deals and opens 1 ♣. North responds 1 ♡. South jumps to 2 NT and bids 3 NT over North's 3 ♡ rebid. West leads the ♠ 4. East has two winning lines of defense. The first is to play the ♠ Q at trick one. This play prevents declarer from holding up his king and keeps the defenders in communication.

Even if East begins with the ♠ A and ♠ Q (and declarer holds off), he still has a chance. When declarer leads his ♡ Q for a finesse, East must duck without batting an eyelash! Unless declarer has a crystal ball, he will repeat the finesse, and now the heart suit will be lost.

QUIZ ON STRATEGY vs. NOTRUMP

1.

♠ A K 2
♡ K 10 2
◇ J 3
♣ Q J 10 8 4

♠ J 4 3
♡ Q 4 3
◇ A K 8 7 4 2
♣ 2

You are defending 3 NT. North opened 1♣, you overcalled 1◇, South bid 2 NT, North raised to 3 NT. Partner leads the ◇9. Plan your defense.

2.

♠ 8 4
♡ 8 6 4
◇ K Q 10 5 4 3
♣ A 2

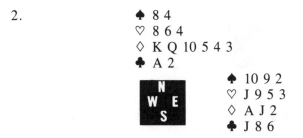

♠ 10 9 2
♡ J 9 5 3
◇ A J 2
♣ J 8 6

You defend 3 NT. South opened 1 NT, and North raised to game. Partner leads the ♠3, and declarer wins your 9 with the jack. Next, declarer leads a diamond to dummy's queen. How do you defend?

3.

♠ K 4
♡ 6 5 4
◇ K 5 4
♣ K J 10 5 4

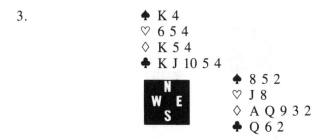

♠ 8 5 2
♡ J 8
◇ A Q 9 3 2
♣ Q 6 2

You defend 3 NT. South opened 1 NT, and North raised to game. Partner leads the ♣J. Declarer wins dummy's king, leads a heart to his ace and passes the ♣9 to your queen. Plan your defense.

4.
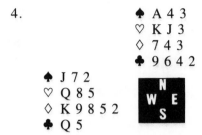

♠ A 4 3
♡ K J 3
◊ 7 4 3
♣ 9 6 4 2

♠ J 7 2
♡ Q 8 5
◊ K 9 8 5 2
♣ Q 5

You defend 3 NT. South opened 1 NT, North raised to 2 NT, South went on to game. You lead the ◊ 5, which goes to partner's jack and declarer's queen. Declarer then leads a heart to the king and a heart back to the 10. You win the queen. How do you defend?

5.

♠ K 3
♡ Q 10 8 4
◊ A 4 2
♣ Q 10 6 3

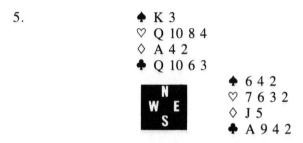

♠ 6 4 2
♡ 7 6 3 2
◊ J 5
♣ A 9 4 2

You defend 3 NT. South opened 1 NT, and North raised to game. Partner leads the ♠Q. Declarer wins in dummy with the king and leads a low club. How do you defend?

6.

♠ 7 5 3
♡ J 8 3
◊ K 10 9 8 5 3
♣ A

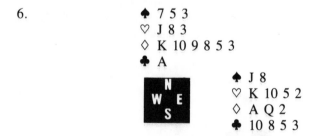

♠ J 8
♡ K 10 5 2
◊ A Q 2
♣ 10 8 5 3

You defend 3 NT. South opened 1 NT, and North raised to game. Partner leads the ♠2, and declarer takes your jack with the king. Declarer then leads the ◊ J, playing low from dummy. You duck, and declarer continues with another diamond, partner discarding. After winning the queen on the second diamond, how do you continue?

SOLUTIONS

1. Duck the first trick. To play the ace, king and another diamond won't help because you have no entry to your long cards. You must keep the partnership communication open. Maybe partner will win a trick with the ♣A or ♣K and will have another diamond to lead. Then you can run your suit.
2. Duck the first diamond. If declarer has two diamonds, this play prevents him from setting up the suit. You retain a *double* stopper while declarer has only one diamond left in his hand. Killing declarer's long suit should be your goal, especially when partner is known to have only four spades.
3. Return a low diamond. Partner is marked with the ♣A, since declarer did not cash that card before finessing for the queen. In that case, partner's spades cannot be as good as A-J-10-x-x — declarer must have the ace as well as the queen. Try to beat the contract with diamond tricks instead of returning partner's lead.
4. *Exit safely* with a heart. With dummy so weak, and with any other return likely to cost a (perhaps crucial) trick, it's time to go passive.
5. Hop up with the ♣A to return partner's suit. You spend your entry early, trying to set up the spades while partner saves his entries.
6. Shift to a club, knocking out declarer's only entry to the diamond suit. Without diamond tricks, his chances of making the contract are slim.

Chapter 4

STRATEGY vs. SUIT CONTRACTS

In this chapter we look at ways the defenders approach their task against a *suit contract*. The objectives are different from notrump. Establishing long cards is less important, since declarer can ruff.

The element of a trump suit makes the play and defense more complex. Declarer has more ways to win tricks and therefore has more options in planning the play. The defenders, in turn, have more possible strategies to counter declarer's plans.

When the defenders see dummy, they must assess its strengths, discern what source of tricks it will provide declarer, and imagine how declarer will conduct the play (and how much success he will have). Depending on dummy's assets, the defenders' approach will vary. We will look at *six* possible defensive strategies against a suit contract. (Only rarely will the right approach fall into no particular category.) Of the six, the first two are the most important.

I. ACTIVE. Suppose you defend 4♠, and dummy is:

♠ A Q x
♡ x x x
♢ x
♣ K Q J 10 x x

How will declarer use this dummy? What tricks will it supply?
It's clear what will happen. Declarer will set up the clubs (if he doesn't already hold the ace) and get plenty of discards for his losers. If you face this imposing dummy, you have no choice — you must *get busy*, going after your tricks before declarer draws trumps and uses the clubs. A heart lead is mandatory. Laying down the ♡ A from A-Q-x or leading from the king or queen is justified. Even if the worst happens, and you lead into the jaws of declarer's A-Q or A-K-J, you lose nothing. Declarer would have thrown his losers on the clubs anyhow. Also, if you hold the ♢ A, you'll cash it before it goes away.

Let's put this concept into a full deal:

1.
```
              ♠ 7
              ♡ A J 6
              ◇ K Q J 10 4
              ♣ A 9 6 3
                              ♠ A 8 5 2
         N                    ♡ K 10 5 3
       W   E                  ◇ 8 5 3
         S                    ♣ 10 4
```

South	West	North	East
3♣	Pass	5♣	(All Pass)

South's 3♣ opening is preemptive, suggesting seven good clubs and little else, and is intended to interfere with *your* bidding. This time, however, North has a good hand and raises to game. West leads the ♠Q, and you take your ace. **What do you lead at trick two?**

Your partner will have the ◇ A, since South would be too strong to preempt with the ♠ K and ◇ A plus his seven good clubs. But the setting trick must come from hearts. *With dummy's diamonds staring you in the face, it's time to get busy.* Shift to a low heart, hoping partner has the queen. Perhaps you can set up a heart trick before declarer sets up the diamonds and throws his heart losers away.

2.

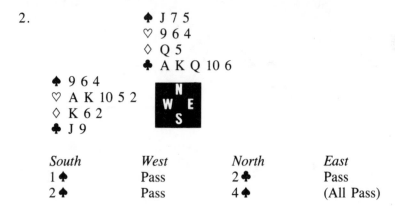

```
              ♠ J 7 5
              ♡ 9 6 4
              ◇ Q 5
              ♣ A K Q 10 6
  ♠ 9 6 4
  ♡ A K 10 5 2
  ◇ K 6 2
  ♣ J 9
```

South	West	North	East
1 ♠	Pass	2 ♣	Pass
2 ♠	Pass	4 ♠	(All Pass)

You cash your top hearts against the 4 ♠ contract, declarer dropping the jack and queen. **What do you do next?**

Again, declarer has the tricks to make his contract unless the defenders take their tricks first. Lead a low diamond, hoping partner has the ace and declarer's hand is something like:

```
  ♠ A K Q x x x
  ♡ Q J
  ◇ J x x
  ♣ x x
```

You won't beat this contract if declarer has the ◇ A. If partner has it, you must cash your diamond tricks without delay, since *dummy's clubs will provide discards.*

II. PASSIVE. *Note well: players often mishandle this type of defense. Failure to understand the active-vs.-passive concept is one of the most common defensive errors.*

Say you are defending 4 ♠ again, but this time dummy is:

♠ Q 6 5
♡ 8 6 4
◊ J 7 5
♣ 9 7 6 3

A sterile dummy is a common sight. **What tricks will this dummy provide?** Right, not much. Dummy has no high-card tricks, no long suit to set up, no ruffing power. When declarer must struggle with a weak dummy, *his losers are unavoidable.* Since declarer can't get rid of his losers, the defenders should *wait* for the tricks they are bound to get sooner or later. Nothing dynamic is required; *aggressive play is avoided.*

This dummy calls for a PASSIVE defense. The passive approach is the antithesis of the busy approach. If you find yourself on lead, try to *exit safely.* Don't take chances and give declarer tricks that aren't his for the taking. A trump lead may be safe — that's probably declarer's strongest suit. A lead from a sequence is safe enough. If declarer leads a suit and you win a trick in it (perhaps after declarer loses a finesse), you might lead the same suit right back; when declarer breaks a suit, to lead it becomes less dangerous.

Another safe way to exit is to lead something that declarer must ruff with a long trump. His trumps will be winners anyway, so you don't mind if he ruffs with one of them.

What you must avoid in a passive defense, however, is getting busy — laying down aces, leading from honors, breaking new suits. You may give declarer a free finesse that he lacks the entries to take, let him avoid a finesse that would have lost, establish intermediate cards for him, eliminate his guesswork and generally make the play easier for him.

3.

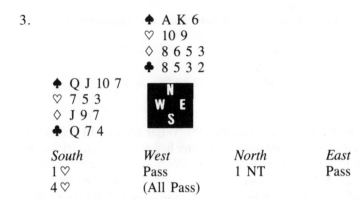

	♠ A K 6		
	♡ 10 9		
	◊ 8 6 5 3		
	♣ 8 5 3 2		

♠ Q J 10 7
♡ 7 5 3
◊ J 9 7
♣ Q 7 4

South	West	North	East
1 ♡	Pass	1 NT	Pass
4 ♡	(All Pass)		

You lead the ♣Q. Declarer takes the top spades in dummy, discarding a low diamond on the second round, and leads a club to his jack and your queen. **What do you lead at this point?**

What is dummy like? Zilch. **Must the defenders hurry to win minor-suit tricks?** No. If declarer has club or diamond losers, he can't get rid of them. **What type of defense does this suggest?** Passive. **What is a safe exit for West at this point?** He should lead a high spade and force declarer to spend a trump. Any other lead may *help declarer*. Declarer's hand could be:

♠ x
♡ A K Q x x x
◊ A Q x
♣ A J 10

A club or diamond return gives him a free finesse, and a heart gives him a dummy entry to take a minor-suit finesse.

4.

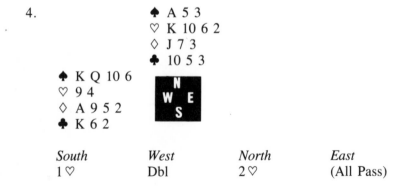

	♠ A 5 3		
	♡ K 10 6 2		
	◊ J 7 3		
	♣ 10 5 3		

♠ K Q 10 6
♡ 9 4
◊ A 9 5 2
♣ K 6 2

South	West	North	East
1 ♡	Dbl	2 ♡	(All Pass)

You lead the ♠K. Declarer wins the ace, draws two rounds of trumps, ending in dummy (East follows), and leads a diamond to his king and your ace. **What do you lead now?**

Since dummy is flat and weak, you should stay *passive*. Just return a diamond. Declarer plays the jack from dummy and partner wins the queen. A spade is returned, and you win the 10 and queen, partner and declarer both following. **What next?**

The dummy is *still* flat and weak, so you need not go looking for club tricks. Lead another diamond instead. Partner plays the 10, and declarer ruffs. Declarer then leads a trump to dummy and a club to his jack. You win your king. *Return a passive club.* Partner plays the 9. Declarer wins the ace but must lose another club to partner's queen in the end. The contract is down one. The full deal:

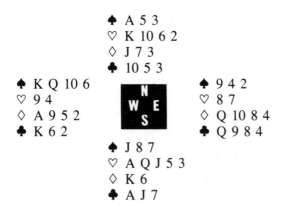

```
                    ♠ A 5 3
                    ♡ K 10 6 2
                    ◊ J 7 3
                    ♣ 10 5 3
     ♠ K Q 10 6                      ♠ 9 4 2
     ♡ 9 4             N             ♡ 8 7
     ◊ A 9 5 2      W     E          ◊ Q 10 8 4
     ♣ K 6 2           S             ♣ Q 9 8 4
                    ♠ J 8 7
                    ♡ A Q J 5 3
                    ◊ K 6
                    ♣ A J 7
```

This is a perfect passive defense. The defenders got out of the lead *safely* every time. (Declarer can do better by *forcing* the defenders to help him. He can, for instance, lead a spade from dummy after drawing trumps. West wins two spade tricks but then must break a minor suit or give declarer a ruff-and-discard with a spade lead.)

Of course, at times you won't be sure whether to get active or go passive. The old standby of counting declarer's tricks may help by telling you whether you need your tricks in a hurry.

Go back to our first problem hand:

(1.)

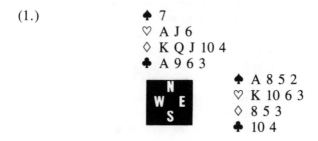

♠ 7
♡ A J 6
◇ K Q J 10 4
♣ A 9 6 3

♠ A 8 5 2
♡ K 10 6 3
◇ 8 5 3
♣ 10 4

South opened 3♣, so he surely had seven club tricks; dummy's diamonds would contribute four tricks, and the ♡A and declarer's ♣K (partner led the ♣Q) were two more. With declarer having material for 13 tricks, the defenders had to get three tricks *quickly*. An active defense was mandatory.

How about this deal from Chapter 1?

5.

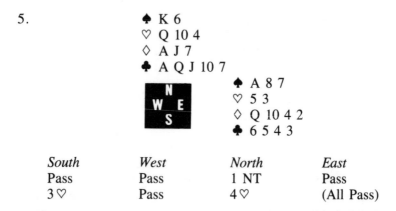

♠ K 6
♡ Q 10 4
◇ A J 7
♣ A Q J 10 7

♠ A 8 7
♡ 5 3
◇ Q 10 4 2
♣ 6 5 4 3

South	West	North	East
Pass	Pass	1 NT	Pass
3 ♡	Pass	4 ♡	(All Pass)

West leads the ♣J. You capture dummy's king with the ace. **What should you lead now?**

Declarer has at least four tricks in clubs, one in diamonds, one in spades. His bidding promises a good five-card heart suit, so he will have at least four tricks there. That's ten tricks, possibly more. So you must get *active* and return a low diamond, hoping partner has the king (plus a trick in trumps).

But . . .

6.

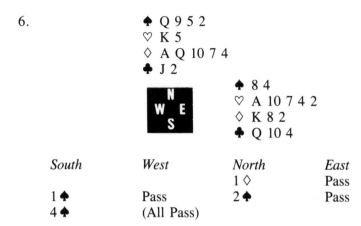

♠ Q 9 5 2
♡ K 5
◊ A Q 10 7 4
♣ J 2

♠ 8 4
♡ A 10 7 4 2
◊ K 8 2
♣ Q 10 4

South	West	North	East
		1 ◊	Pass
1 ♠	Pass	2 ♠	Pass
4 ♠	(All Pass)		

West leads the ♡Q. This wins the first trick, but declarer ruffs the next heart. Declarer draws two rounds of trumps, partner's jack falling on the second round, and then rides the ◊9 to your king. **What should you lead now?**

Declarer has five spade tricks and four diamonds. That's nine. *He cannot make the contract without a trick in clubs.* Since declarer must lead clubs himself sooner or later, you don't have to do his work for him. Get out passively with a diamond. If you lead clubs instead, and declarer's clubs are headed by the king, he can make an impossible contract by playing low. Partner has to win the ace, establishing declarer's king as the tenth trick.

Several other strategies are available to the defenders. For example . . .

III. LEADING TRUMPS. Suppose the contract is the usual 4 ♠, and dummy is:

♠ Q x x
♡ x
◊ x x x x x
♣ J x x x

What source of tricks does this dummy contain? Obviously, declarer can use this dummy only for *ruffing* tricks. If he has losing hearts, he will try to ruff them. The defenders should lead trumps, hoping to strand declarer with his losers. Drawing two of declarer's trumps for the price of one is the right approach when declarer can take extra tricks by using his trumps separately.

7.

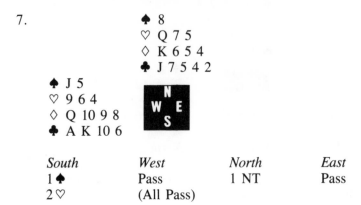

♠ 8
♥ Q 7 5
♦ K 6 5 4
♣ J 7 5 4 2

♠ J 5
♥ 9 6 4
♦ Q 10 9 8
♣ A K 10 6

South	West	North	East
1 ♣	Pass	1 NT	Pass
2 ♥	(All Pass)		

You lead the ♣A, winning the first trick. **What next?**

Dummy's ♦K may be a trick, but you can't help that. However, declarer will probably want to ruff spades in dummy (in fact, declarer may play the entire hand as a crossruff if he is short in clubs) and you can reduce dummy's ruffing power. Shift to a trump at trick two.

Note that your partner probably has five spades, so declarer may well have losing spades to ruff. And dummy has no other source of tricks for you to worry about. (As we will see in the next chapter West might have led a trump *at trick one*, anticipating the dummy from the bidding.)

Now for some rare strategies vs. suit contracts:

IV. FORCING DEFENSE

In a *forcing* defense, you make declarer *lose control* of the play by forcing him to ruff so many times that he runs out of trumps! This approach is attractive when a defender has unexpected length in trumps — usually four cards or more.

To force declarer, you usually start by leading your *longest* suit. Maybe declarer is short there and will soon have to ruff. In this deal your long suit is strong, increasing your chance of success.

8.

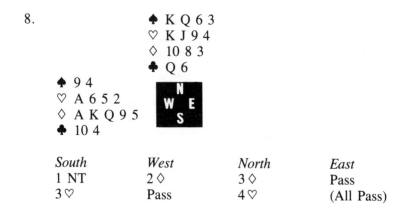

♠ K Q 6 3
♡ K J 9 4
◇ 10 8 3
♣ Q 6

♠ 9 4
♡ A 6 5 2
◇ A K Q 9 5
♣ 10 4

South	West	North	East
1 NT	2 ◇	3 ◇	Pass
3 ♡	Pass	4 ♡	(All Pass)

North's 3 ◇ cuebid was a form of the *Stayman convention*. You lead three top diamonds, and declarer ruffs the third round. Declarer next leads a trump. **How do you plan the defense?**

You know declarer is playing a 4-4 trump fit, and your four trumps may be a nuisance. You already forced declarer to ruff in his hand, so if you can shorten *dummy*, declarer will be out of control — you'll have more trumps than he has in either hand.

To force dummy, you must wait until declarer is out of trumps in his hand. Therefore, when declarer leads a trump to the king and a trump back to his queen, you must *duck* both times. (If you mistakenly win and lead another diamond, declarer can ruff in his hand, preserving dummy's trump length and keeping control.) If declarer leads a third trump, you win, and *now* a diamond lead accomplishes your goal by forcing dummy to ruff. You'll be left in control with your last trump.

(A good declarer will abandon trumps after he sees the 4-1 trump break. He will lead black-suit winners, letting West score a low heart for down one, but keeping control and avoiding down two.)

Conceding a *ruff-and-discard* can cost the defense a trick, but if declarer has no losers that a ruff-and-discard will let him avoid, it may be an effective way to attack his trump holding. In the problem above, if dummy were:

♠ K Q 6 3
♡ K J 9 4
◇ 10 8
♣ Q 6 2,

West should still lead three rounds of diamonds, even if declarer gets a ruff-and-discard. On the bidding, declarer has all the missing high cards, so a ruff-and-discard can't help him and may weaken his trumps.

One word of caution. Occasionally, a persistent forcing defense may help declarer by letting him score several low trumps that otherwise would not win tricks. The objective of a forcing defense is to make it impossible for declarer to draw trumps so he can't use his side suits. Beware of a forcing defense if your trump holding is very long *and strong*, or if declarer has fast side-suit tricks he can cash without drawing trumps.

V. TRYING FOR RUFFS

Like many players, you may be fond of this approach. If you have a side-suit singleton, it hits the table at almost the speed of light. You just know partner will produce the ace and return the suit for you to ruff. You like leading doubletons almost as much. Perhaps, then, we should emphasize when you *shouldn't* try for a ruff by leading from shortness.

---

(1) When you have *natural trump tricks*.
(2) When you have *great length* in trumps. Even if a ruff is available, a forcing defense may work better. (Rare exception: Try for ruffs when you fear that declarer may be able to *endplay you in trumps*.)
(3) When you have a *strong hand*. If partner's hand is weak, he may never get in to give you your ruff.
(4) When declarer can probably *draw trumps* before you get a ruff. (However, if you hold the trump ace or king — a fast reentry — your chances of getting a ruff are much better.)
(5) When the contract will be defeated anyway if partner has a trick. Look at this situation:

You, West, hold:

9.
♠ 10 7 5 3
♥ A K 4
♦ 9 7 5 4 2
♣ 4

South	West	North	East
		1 ♣	Pass
1 ♥	Pass	2 ♥	Pass
3 ♣	Pass	4 ♥	Pass
5 ♥	(All Pass)		

What is your lead?

To lead your singleton club would be misguided. If partner has the ♣A (or the king behind the ace), the contract will always fail. But partner is much more likely, on this bidding, to hold Q-x-x or J-10-x-x, in which case a club lead may pick up his holding for declarer.

A *risk* always goes with leading from shortness. Your short suit may be the opponents' long suit — a suit they will use for tricks. Leading the suit may help them establish it. Therefore, risk a short-suit lead only when conditions look right.

VI. EXTRA TRUMP TRICKS

It's often hard to imagine winning tricks in the opponents' best suit. Nevertheless, an UPPERCUT or TRUMP PROMOTION may be your only chance to defeat the contract.

In an *uppercut* a defender ruffs with an intermediate card, forcing declarer to weaken his trumps by spending a high trump to overruff.

A TRUMP PROMOTION MAY BE THE ONLY WAY
TO DEFEAT THE CONTRACT.

10.
♠ A K 6 3
♡ 5
◇ 9 6 2
♣ A K Q 7 3

♠ 10 5
♡ A 9 2
◇ K Q 10 8 5 3
♣ 9 4

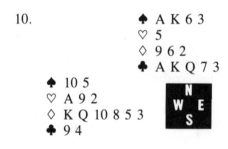

South	West	North	East
2♡ (1)	Pass	2 NT	Pass
3♡ (2)	Pass	4♡	(All Pass)

(1) Weak two-bid
(2) No side ace or king

You lead the ◇K. Partner overtakes and returns a diamond. Declarer follows with the jack the second time. **How do you defend?**
No more side-suit tricks are available, so the trump suit offers the

only chance for a fourth trick. At trick three lead a *low* diamond, forcing partner to ruff. He ruffs with the ♡7, and declarer overruffs with the 10. Your ♡9 begins to look better. When declarer leads the ♡K, you grab your ace and lead a fourth diamond. This time partner ruffs with the 8. When declarer must overruff with another honor, your 9 is suddenly worth a trick! The other hands are:

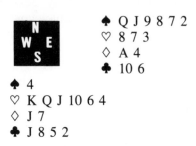

```
                    ♠ Q J 9 8 7 2
      N             ♡ 8 7 3
  W       E         ◊ A 4
      S             ♣ 10 6
♠ 4
♡ K Q J 10 6 4
◊ J 7
♣ J 8 5 2
```

An important part of this strategy is that *the defense must cash their side winners before attacking declarer's trump holding*; otherwise, declarer may survive with a *loser-on-loser* play.

In the last deal, if *West* had the ♠A instead of dummy, he would need to cash it before leading a third round of diamonds. If he did not, declarer would discard his losing spade instead of overruffing East at the cost of a trump honor.

The position below illustrates a TRUMP PROMOTION.

```
              ♡ 3 2
  ♡ Q 9 7 4              ♡ 8
              ♡ A K J 10 6 5
```

Hearts is trumps. East leads a diamond, in which both West and declarer are void. Declarer ruffs with the ♡J. West should *decline to overruff,* and now his trump holding is worth *two* tricks. (It is seldom right to overruff with a natural trump winner, as the ♡Q is here. If you save your trumps, their value may increase.)

Let's review the six types of defenses to suit contracts. Remember, above all, that a good defender knows when he must take tricks in a hurry and when he can wait patiently for his tricks.

1. *ACTIVE,* indicated if dummy (or perhaps declarer) has a long, strong side suit that will provide *discards.*
2. *PASSIVE,* indicated if dummy lacks trick-taking power and declarer will have trouble avoiding losers.
3. *TRUMP LEADS,* indicated if dummy's only source of tricks is ruffing power.
4. *FORCING,* in which the defenders make declarer ruff so many times that he runs out of trumps and can't use his side suits. This defense is attractive when a defender has extra length in trumps.
5. *TRYING FOR RUFFS,* best when (1) you have trump control, and (2) your partner has an entry to give you a ruff.
6. *EXTRA TRUMP TRICKS.* In an *uppercut,* a defender ruffs with an intermediate trump, forcing declarer to weaken his trump holding by overruffing. In a *trump promotion,* declarer must either ruff low and be overruffed or ruff high at the cost of strengthening a defender's trump holding. Winning unexpected trump tricks may be the defenders' only chance.

1.
                   ♠ K 10 3 2
                   ♡ A 7 5
                   ◇ Q 8 4
                   ♣ A J 3

♠ Q 7 5
♡ K Q J 2
◇ K 9 3
♣ 8 6 4

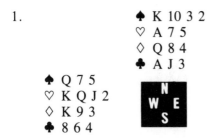

You are defending 2 ♠. North opened 1 ♣, South bid 1 ♠, North raised. Declarer wins your ♡ K with the ace and leads the ♠ K and a spade to the jack. You win the queen and cash the ♡ Q and ♡ J, all following. How do you continue?

2.
                   ♠ A Q
                   ♡ J 9 6 4
                   ◇ A J 3
                   ♣ K 7 5 2

♠ 8 4
♡ K Q 5
◇ K 10 5 2
♣ Q J 10 8

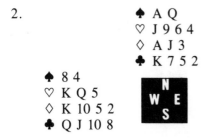

You defend 4 ♡. Dummy opened 1 NT, declarer responded 3 ♠ and converted 3 NT to 4 ♡. Your ♣ Q holds the first trick, but declarer ruffs the next club. He leads a spade to the ace and finesses the ♡ J to your queen. What do you lead?

3.
                   ♠ A K 2
                   ♡ 10 9 8
                   ◇ 10 6 2
                   ♣ Q 10 8 7

♠ 4 3
♡ A 7 6 5
◇ K J 9 7 5
♣ 6 5

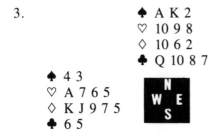

You defend 4 ♡. Declarer opened 1 ♡, dummy raised and declarer went on to game. You lead a diamond to partner's ace. He cashes the ◇ Q and leads a third diamond, ruffed by declarer. Declarer now leads the ♡ K. How do you defend?

4.

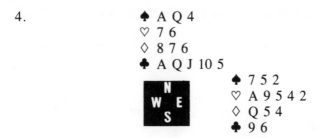

♠ A Q 4
♥ 7 6
♦ 8 7 6
♣ A Q J 10 5

♠ 7 5 2
♥ A 9 5 4 2
♦ Q 5 4
♣ 9 6

You defend 4 ♠. Declarer opened 1 ♠, dummy responded 2 ♣ and raised declarer's 2 ♠ rebid to game. Partner leads the ♥Q. How do you defend?

5.

♠ 7 6 3 2
♥ A J 3 2
♦ 3
♣ 10 9 8 7

♠ K Q 10 5
♥ Q 10 9 8
♦ Q 9
♣ 6 5 4

You defend 2 ♣. Declarer opened 1 ♦, dummy responded 1 ♥ and passed declarer's 2 ♣ rebid. Your ♠K holds the first trick, partner playing the 9 and declarer the jack. What do you do now?

6.

♠ A K 3
♥ 3
♦ J 7 6 5
♣ A Q 6 5 4

♠ 6 5 4
♥ A 9 2
♦ 9 8
♣ 10 8 7 3 2

You defend 4 ♥. Your partner opened 1 ♦, and declarer preempted with 4 ♥. Partner overtakes your ♦9 lead with the 10 and cashes the queen. On the ♦K, declarer ruffs with the ♥K. How do you defend?

7.

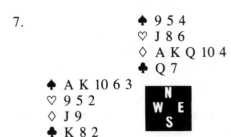

♠ 9 5 4
♡ J 8 6
◇ A K Q 10 4
♣ Q 7

♠ A K 10 6 3
♡ 9 5 2
◇ J 9
♣ K 8 2

You defend 4 ♡. Declarer opened 1 ♡, you overcalled 1 ♠. Dummy bid 2 ◇ and raised declarer's 2 ♡ rebid to game. You cash the ♠ A and ♣ K, declarer following with the jack and queen. What do you lead at trick three?

8. You, West, hold:

♠ A Q 7 5 3
♡ A K 5
◇ 10 9 7 4
♣ 2

South	West	North	East
1 ♡	1 ♠	2 ♣	Pass
3 ♣	Pass	3 ♡	Pass
4 ♡	(All Pass)		

What is your opening lead?

SOLUTIONS

1. Go *passive* by returning your last trump. With dummy so weak, your minor-suit tricks aren't going anywhere. Let declarer break the minor suits.

2. Get *active* with a diamond return, hoping to set up a trick if partner has the queen. If you don't lead a diamond now, declarer will have time to draw trumps and discard dummy's diamonds on his spades. If he has a losing diamond, he will then ruff it in dummy.

3. Hold up your ace of trumps until dummy has none left. Then you can force declarer to ruff another diamond lead *in his hand.* If he started with only five trumps, he will lose control — you will have a long trump and a good diamond. If declarer stops playing trumps after seeing the 4-1 split, he can keep control by cashing his black-suit winners and forcing *you* to ruff with your low trump. Nevertheless, you get four tricks.

4. Win the ♡ A and shift to the ◇ Q. You need three *fast* diamond tricks to beat the contract, and partner must therefore hold A-J-10. If you lead a low diamond instead, declarer will play low, ducking the trick safely to partner and losing only two diamonds.

5. Shift to trumps to cut down on dummy's only source of tricks. (You also keep declarer from ruffing spades in his hand.)

6. You should *discard* on the third diamond. If partner has a trump as high as the 10, your A-9-2 will then be worth *two* tricks. If you overruff the ♡ K with your ace, you are letting declarer force out your ace with his king, which he intended to do anyway. It is seldom right to overruff with a natural trump winner. Let your trumps increase in value.

7. Shift to a club, hoping declarer's hand is something like:

   ♠ Q J
   ♡ A K Q x x x
   ◇ x x
   ♣ J x x

   You can't beat the contract if declarer holds the ♣ A.

8. Lead the ◇ 10. Avoid leading your club singleton, since the contract will always be defeated if partner has the ♣ A. If, as is far more likely, he has the ♣ Q or ♣ J, a club lead will help declarer.

Chapter 5

EDUCATED GUESSING ON OPENING LEAD

Opening leads may be the hardest part of defense. Even a fine defender will lose a trick, or even the contract, on opening lead occasionally — some degree of guesswork is always present. On opening lead, you see only your own cards. Nobody can tell how the other cards will lie and how the play will develop. Nevertheless, it is possible to make an *educated guess* on opening lead.

Bridge books usually provide a table of holdings with suggested leads (for instance, lead the *10* from Q-10-9-8). These books may mention specific holdings that make attractive leads. However, general advice in picking an opening lead is worth little. A card that would be a good lead in one situation may be ill-advised in another. Let's say you hold these cards on three consecutive deals:

♠ J 10 9
♡ K J 9 2
♢ A 5 3 2
♣ 9 5

On each deal you are opening leader. Obviously, you can't decide without knowing the bidding. If right-hand opponent bid hearts, for example, a heart lead would always be unattractive. The bidding could have gone:

LHO	RHO		LHO	RHO
	1 ♠			1 ♡
2 ♢	2 ♠	or	1 NT	2 ♣
4 ♠	Pass		Pass	

		LHO	RHO
			1 ♣
or		1 ♡	3 ♣
		Pass	

and three different opening leads would be proper.

*YOU HAVE MANY CHOICES AVAILABLE WHEN
YOU'RE THE OPENING LEADER.*

Let's see how a good player picks a lead by *listening* to the bidding and *looking* at his own hand. Then we can come back to these deals and choose the best lead in each case.

In the last two chapters we discussed possible strategies the defenders can adopt after they see dummy's strengths and weaknesses. Even though you can't see dummy, the opening lead is the first step in your defensive strategy. *When you make the opening lead, you are trying to intitiate the right strategy before you see dummy.* This isn't as hard as it sounds. The bidding will often paint a clear picture: whether dummy will be weak or strong, balanced or shapely. Opening leads require imagination. You must *visualize* dummy and foresee how declarer will use dummy's assets. If you can anticipate how the play will develop, you will have a head start in countering declarer's plans.

Some examples will make the idea clear. Try your imagination in these situations.

1.		LHO	RHO
	♠ K J x		
	♡ x x		1 ♡
	◊ J 10 8 x x	2 ♣	2 ♡
	♣ Q x x	4 ♡	Pass

What sort of dummy do you expect? Dummy will be fairly strong, won't it? Even though opener showed a minimum, responder went to game — responder has an opening bid or better himself. Dummy will have heart support and a club suit — maybe a good suit, since responder took the trouble to show it.

How will the play go in 4♡? How will declarer try to make his contract? What tricks will dummy provide? Dummy's clubs will probably be a source of tricks. Declarer will set up the clubs and throw away his spade and diamond losers. Look at *your* club holding. **Will declarer be successful if he tries to set up dummy's clubs?** How do you like your ♣Q-x-x in front of dummy's suit? It looks ominous, doesn't it? If declarer finesses against the queen, his finesse will work like a charm. If he tries to set up the clubs with a ruff, that will work too — the suit is divided evenly.

Clearly, declarer has the material for at least 10 tricks. (The situation would be more hopeful if you had only one club or five clubs; then dummy's suit wouldn't be as threatening.) **What's the best strategy when dummy has a side suit that will provide discards?** Active. You must get busy and win fast tricks before declarer discards his losers.

The crucial question: **What is your most aggressive lead?** A spade! Lead low, since you are hoping partner can contribute the ace or queen to the trick. If partner has the ♣A, you may take two or three tricks immediately; if he has the ♣Q, you establish a trick or two. Remember, you need tricks *in a hurry*. Given time, declarer will discard his losers.

Some players hate to lead from a king. A famous bridge authority once taught his students *never* to lead from kings. (We've always thought that, if there were any justice, he would spend eternity on opening lead with a hand with all four kings!) Sometimes it is more dangerous *not* to lead from a king. If you need fast tricks, lead from your strength. On this deal, if you lead a spade into the jaws of the A-Q, you may have lost nothing. Declarer would throw his ♠Q on the clubs anyway. But if *partner* has a spade honor, you *must* lead spades *now*.

2.	♠ A Q 10 8	*LHO*	*RHO*
	♡ x x x		1♠
	◊ J 10 9 x	1 NT	2♡
	♣ A x	Pass	

DUMMY: Bad hand. No good side suit that declarer can set up. Doesn't like spades (will often have singleton or void), likes hearts.

HOW THE PLAY WILL GO: Declarer will ruff spades in dummy. You know he has losing spades because your spades are strong, and he can't get rid of his spades in any other way.

STRATEGY: Lead trumps to protect your good spades.

SUGGESTED OPENING LEAD: Trump

3.

		LHO	*RHO*
♠	K x x		1♡
♡	x x x	2♡	Pass
◊	J 10 9 x		
♣	A x x		

DUMMY: Weak. 6-9 points. A good side suit is unlikely. Heart support.

HOW THE PLAY WILL GO: Unknown, but declarer will have his work cut out. He has limited values and will have trouble taking tricks, especially if you don't help him by leading from kings and snatching aces.

STRATEGY: Go passive and let declarer struggle.

SUGGESTED OPENING LEAD: ◊J or a trump. Contrast this situation with the first one, where you must take advantage of being on lead to set up tricks quickly. Here, the contract is only 2♡, and your side will get to lead several times. You can get busy later if necessary.

4.

		LHO	*RHO*
♠	J 10 8 x x		1♣
♡	K x x	2◊	3♣
◊	x x x	6♣	Pass
♣	A x		

DUMMY: Super hand with good diamonds and a club fit.

HOW THE PLAY WILL GO: Once declarer draws trumps, dummy's diamonds will provide all the tricks he needs.

STRATEGY: Active

SUGGESTED OPENING LEAD: Low heart

5.　♠ A x x x　　*LHO*　　*RHO*
　　♡ x x　　　　　　　　1♠
　　◊ K J 9 x x　　2♡　　2♠
　　♣ K x　　　　　3♠　　Pass

DUMMY:　　　10-12 HCP, five or more hearts, spade support.
HOW THE PLAY WILL GO: Not clear, but if declarer wants to use
　　　　　　　dummy's hearts, he must draw trumps first. Your
　　　　　　　unexpected length in trumps may be a nuisance.
STRATEGY:　Forcing game
SUGGESTED OPENING LEAD: Low diamond

6.　♠ x x x　　　*LHO*　　*RHO*
　　♡ K 10 x x　　　　　　1♠
　　◊ J 10 9 x　　2♠　　2 NT
　　♣ K x　　　　　3♠　　Pass

DUMMY:　　　Anemic. Closer to 6 points, since responder declined
　　　　　　　opener's try for game. Distributional, since responder
　　　　　　　preferred spades to notrump.
HOW THE PLAY WILL GO: Having promised ruffing power and
　　　　　　　little else, dummy will provide declarer with extra
　　　　　　　trump tricks.
STRATEGY:　Trump leads
SUGGESTED OPENING LEAD: Trump

7.　♠ x x x　　　*LHO*　　*RHO*
　　♡ K Q 10 x　　　　　　1 NT
　　◊ A Q x x x　　2♣　　2♠
　　♣ x　　　　　　4♠　　Pass

DUMMY:　　　Four or more spades, 9-14 HCP.
HOW THE PLAY WILL GO: Unclear
STRATEGY:　There isn't one you could bet on, but you should *not*
　　　　　　　lead your singleton. Partner has a weak hand and
　　　　　　　will never win a trick to give you the ruff you seek.
　　　　　　　A club lead could help *declarer* if partner has Q-x-x
　　　　　　　or J-10-x-x.
SUGGESTED OPENING LEAD: ♡K

Suppose your hand is (same auction):

♠ A x x
♡ x x x x
◇ J x x x x
♣ x

Now a singleton lead is perfect. Since you have a weak hand, partner will have an entry. Your trump ace means that declarer can't draw trumps without letting you back in for a second chance at your ruff.

8. ♠ J 10 9 x
    ♡ A x
    ◇ x x x
    ♣ A x x x

	LHO	RHO
		1♡
	2♣	3♣
	3♡	4♡
	Pass	

DUMMY: Club suit, heart fit, at least invitational values.
HOW THE PLAY WILL GO: Beautifully for your side, if you make the right lead.
STRATEGY: Trying for ruffs (in partner's hand).
SUGGESTED OPENING LEAD: ♣A, hoping partner has a singleton or void and can ruff the next club lead. It pays to *listen to the bidding*.

Next, we will look at opening leads against notrump. The usual strategy is to establish a long suit, but occasional exceptions arise.

9. ♠ x x x
    ♡ A 10 x x x
    ◇ K x x
    ♣ J x

	LHO	RHO
		1 NT
	3 NT	Pass

Lead your fourth-highest heart. You have a decent suit plus a couple of possible entries.

10. ♠ x x x
    ♡ J 10
    ◇ 10 x x x x
    ♣ J x x

	LHO	RHO
		1 NT
	3 NT	Pass

This time you have less reason to lead your long suit. Since you have no entry, you will never get to cash long cards even if you establish them. Lead the ♡ J, hoping to set up *partner's* most likely suit. Note that the opponents made no attempt to play in hearts (responder didn't use *Stayman*), so partner probably has heart length.

11.	♠ A K x x x	*LHO*	*RHO*
	♡ x x		1 NT
	◇ J x x	3 NT	Pass
	♣ x x x		

With no entry outside spades, lead a low spade. You hope to keep communication with partner's hand.

12.	♠ Q 10 x x	*LHO*	*RHO*
	♡ A x x		1 NT
	◇ x x	3 NT	Pass
	♣ Q 10 x x		

The opponents' lack of interest in a major-suit contract should influence you to lead a spade rather than a club.

13.	♠ A 10 x x	*LHO*	*RHO*
	♡ Q x x x		1 NT
	◇ 10 9 7	4 NT	6 NT
	♣ Q x	Pass	

Since partner has no points, it would be dangerous to lead from a queen or cash the ♠ A. Lead the ◇ 10, hoping one of your queens will take a trick. Against 6 NT or any grand slam, a passive lead is usually best. Establishing a long suit is not a priority when you need only two tricks to beat the contract.

14.	♠ x x	*LHO*	*RHO*
	♡ K J 9 x x		1 ♡
	◇ 10 9 x	1 ♠	1 NT
	♣ Q x x	3 NT	Pass

Lead the ◇ 10. You cannot establish heart tricks when declarer probably has five hearts, and a heart lead may give away a trick.

15.	♠ x x	*LHO*	*RHO*
	♡ Q 9 x x		1 ♣
	◊ J 9 x	1 ♠	1 NT
	♣ K J 9 x	2 NT	Pass

This is the time for a passive lead. The auction suggests that the opponents have no extra strength. You have declarer's clubs bottled up, and partner is marked with at least four spades. You may not need to set up a suit to beat the contract. Declarer may go down on his own when he runs out of tricks. The downside to a heart lead: in setting up your suit, you may give up a crucial trick.

Remember the idea behind choosing an opening lead. Look at your own cards, listen to the opponents' bidding and decide how declarer will conduct the play. Then apply your strategy, commencing with the opening lead. With practice and experience, your opening leads will improve.

Can you pick the best opening lead on the three deals at the beginning of the chapter?

1. ♡ 2 (Active defense).
2. Trump (Stop heart ruffs in dummy).
3. ♠ J (Passive).

Summary:
To make effective opening leads:

Remember that the opening lead is the first step in applying an overall defensive strategy.

Listen to the bidding. Visualize the dummy and imagine how declarer will use it to try for his contract.

Look at your own hand. Does anything about it indicate whether declarer's probable line of play will succeed?

Apply the appropriate strategy, beginning with the opening lead, to counter declarer's plans.

Against suit contracts:

If your strategy is:	Your opening lead will be:
ACTIVE	AGGRESSIVE. Lead from honors or lay down aces.
PASSIVE	SAFE. Lead trumps or lead from a sequence.
PREVENTING RUFFS	A TRUMP, drawing two of declarer's trumps for one of yours.
THE FORCING GAME	YOUR LONGEST SUIT.
TRYING FOR RUFFS	FROM SHORTNESS. Rarely, you may lead a suit *partner* may be short in.
EXTRA TRUMP TRICKS	FROM SHORTNESS OR LENGTH. A short-suit lead may result in a trump promotion; a long-suit lead may result in an uppercut.

Against notrump contracts:

If your strategy is:	Your opening lead will be:
ACTIVE	YOUR LONGEST SUIT or partner's long suit.
PASSIVE	SAFE. Lead through dummy's bid suit or lead from a sequence.
KILLING A SUIT	The suit that contains an entry to declarer's (or dummy's) long suit.

QUIZ ON OPENING LEADS

1.	♠ x x	*LHO*	*RHO*
	♡ K J 9 x x	1♡	1♠
	◇ A x	2♡	3♠
	♣ Q J 9 x	4♠	Pass

2.	♠ A x x x	*LHO*	*RHO*
	♡ x		1♣
	◇ K Q 10 x x	1♡	1♠
	♣ Q x x	3♠	4♠
		Pass	

3.	♠ 10 x	*LHO*	*RHO*
	♡ Q x x		1♠
	◇ J 10 9 x	2♡	2♠
	♣ K 10 8 x	3♠	4♠
		Pass	

4.	♠ 9 x	*LHO*	*RHO*
	♡ K x x		1 NT
	◇ J x x x	2♣	2♡
	♣ 10 9 8 x	4♡	Pass

5.	♠ K J 9 x	*LHO*	*RHO*
	♡ A x		1♠
	◇ x x x x	1 NT	2◇
	♣ Q 9 x	Pass	

6.	♠ x x	*LHO*	*RHO*
	♡ Q 10 x x		1♠
	◇ K J x x	2♣	2♡
	♣ J x x	2♠	3♠
		4♠	Pass

7.	♠ 10 x	*LHO*	*RHO*
	♡ Q 10 x x x	1◇	1♡
	◇ x x x x	2◇	3 NT
	♣ 10 x		

8. ♠ A 10 9 x
   ♡ x
   ◇ Q J 10 x
   ♣ J x x x

LHO	RHO
	1♠
2♡	2♠
3♠	Pass

9. ♠ K Q x x
   ♡ x
   ◇ K J x x x
   ♣ A J x

You	LHO	Partner	RHO
			1♡
Dbl	Pass	Pass	Pass

10. ♠ Q J x x
    ♡ x x
    ◇ A Q 10 x
    ♣ x x x

LHO	RHO
1♠	2♣
2♡	2 NT
3♣	4♣
5♣	Pass

11. ♠ x x
    ♡ J 10 9 x
    ◇ Q J 10 x
    ♣ K x x

LHO	RHO
1◇	1♠
2♠	Pass

12. ♠ J 10 x
    ♡ K 10 x
    ◇ K 9 x x
    ♣ x x x

You	LHO	Partner	RHO
		1♠	2♣
2♠	3♣	4♠	5♣
Dbl	Pass	Pass	Pass

13. ♠ 10 x x
    ♡ x x
    ◇ Q J x x
    ♣ K J 9 x

You	LHO	Partner	RHO
	1♣	1♠	2♡
Pass	3♡	Pass	3 NT
Pass	4♡	Pass	Pass
Pass			

14. ♠ K x x x x
    ♡ Q x
    ◇ x x x
    ♣ x x x

You	LHO	Partner	RHO
		1♠	Pass
2♠	Dbl	3♠	4♡
Pass	Pass	Pass	

15. ♠ K 10 x
    ♡ K 10 x x
    ◇ x
    ♣ x x x x x

LHO	RHO
1◇	1♡
3◇	3♡
3♠	3 NT
Pass	

16.   ♠ J x x x   *LHO*   *RHO*
      ♡ 10 x   1 ◊
      ◊ Q 10 x x   1 ♡   1 NT
      ♣ K x x   2 NT   Pass

17.   ♠ A K 9 5 2   *LHO*   *RHO*
      ♡ x x x   1 NT
      ◊ Q x   3 NT   Pass
      ♣ A x x

SOLUTIONS

1.   ♣Q. Go passive, since you have dummy's long suit under control. You need not lay down the ◊A — declarer can't throw diamonds on dummy's hearts. Partner is unlikely to have the ◊K anyway, on the bidding.
2.   ◊K. Try for a forcing game with your four trumps.
3.   Club. Get active. Dummy has a heart suit, and your ♡Q is poorly placed.
4.   ♠9. Try for a ruff with a bad hand plus trump control.
5.   Trump. Declarer will need spade ruffs in dummy.
6.   Diamond. Although you have declarer's second suit under control, dummy has a side suit. Stopping heart ruffs in dummy is less important than getting your diamond trick(s) before declarer sets up the clubs for discards.
7.   ♣10. Try to hit partner's suit, since declarer bid your suit and you have no entries. Partner is more likely to have clubs than spades. He is marked with a few points and he might have overcalled 1♠ with a decent suit. A 2♣ overcall, however, would have been riskier.
8.   ◊Q. Leading your singleton is pointless when you have sure trump tricks anyway.
9.   Trump. This is an odd variation on leading trumps. Partner must have a solid trump holding to convert your takeout double to penalty. If you lead trumps right away, you can stop declarer from winning tricks with low trumps.
10.   Trump. The bidding marks dummy with diamond shortness, and declarer has diamond length. You don't have to fear that declarer will take tricks with dummy's spade suit.
11.   ♡J. The normal, passive lead, with dummy known to have a minimum opening.

12. Trump. The opponents have sacrificed against your game. Since partner has a good hand, your side surely has most of the high-card strength. By leading trumps, you may stop declarer from ruffing losers, and there is no rush for you to do anything else.

13. Trump. Since you have good intermediates in clubs and diamonds, declarer's most likely source of extra tricks is spade ruffs in dummy. Dummy promised ruffing potential by converting 3 NT to hearts.

14. ♠K. Make an exception to the principle of leading low in partner's suit. If you *hold the first trick*, perhaps you can make an effective switch through dummy to partner's side strength.

15. ♠K. Imaginative. You hope to knock the ♠A out of dummy so declarer can't use it as a late entry to the diamonds.

16. ♡10. Passive. You have good diamonds, partner is marked with at least four hearts and the opponents have nothing extra in high cards.

17. ♠2. You have no reason to show count by leading fourth best, since partner will never win a trick. You may fool declarer, though. (For instance, he may think it's safe to knock out your ♣A.)

Chapter 6

DEFENSIVE SIGNALS

Let's begin with three common defensive dilemmas.

I.

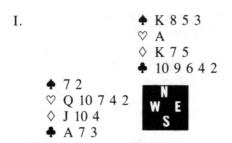

♠ K 8 5 3
♥ A
⋄ K 7 5
♣ 10 9 6 4 2

♠ 7 2
♥ Q 10 7 4 2
⋄ J 10 4
♣ A 7 3

South opens 1 NT, North raises to 3 NT. You lead the ♥4, won by dummy's ace. Declarer then leads a club from dummy, putting up the queen from his hand, and you win the ace. **What do you do now?** This is an uncomfortable situation. Declarer could have either:

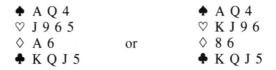

♠ A Q 4		♠ A Q 4
♥ J 9 6 5	or	♥ K J 9 6
⋄ A 6		⋄ 8 6
♣ K Q J 5		♣ K Q J 5

You must continue hearts in the first case and shift to your ⋄J in the second.

II.

♠ 7 6 5
♥ Q 5
⋄ 8 7 6
♣ K Q J 10 3

♠ Q 10 8 4 2
♥ K 6 4
⋄ Q 5
♣ A 8 6

South opens 1 NT, North raises to 2 NT, South goes on to 3 NT. West leads the ♥10, covered by the queen, king and ace. Declarer then leads a club toward dummy. Do you see the problem? You must take your ♣ A just as declarer plays the last club from his hand. Then declarer will get only as many club tricks as he deserves. **But how many clubs does declarer have?** Two, three or four?

III.

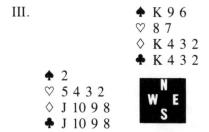

```
           ♠ K 9 6
           ♡ 8 7
           ◊ K 4 3 2
           ♣ K 4 3 2
 ♠ 2
 ♡ 5 4 3 2          N
 ◊ J 10 9 8     W       E
 ♣ J 10 9 8         S
```

South opens 1 ♡, North responds 1 NT; South jumps to 3 ♡, North raises to 4 ♡. You lead your singleton spade. Partner wins the ace and returns a spade. **What do you lead after ruffing?** You would like to give partner the lead if possible to give you another ruff.

Three kinds of defensive signals exist, each designed to handle one of those three nightmare problems. Here they are.

I. *ATTITUDE.* The defenders' most frequent problem is choosing a suit to lead (or deciding whether to keep leading a suit). Therefore, the *attitude* signal, which shows liking or dislike for a suit, is the most important signal. A defender usually shows attitude as *his partner leads* a suit. He may also show attitude in *discarding*.

> The play of a *high* spot encourages. The play of a *low* spot denies interest (and may, under some circumstances, demand a shift).

Let's look at the first problem again and see how attitude helps the defenders. The heart position was:

```
                ♡ A
 ♡ Q 10 7 4 2    ■      ♡ K 8 3 or ♡ 8 5 3 ?
                ♡ J 9 6 5 or ♡ K J 9 6?
```

West leads the ♡4, and dummy's ace wins. *East should signal attitude in following suit.* With K-8-3, he would play his 8, an *encouraging* spot, suggesting strength in hearts and begging for more heart leads. With 8-5-3, East would play the 3, his *lowest* spot. From his point of view, further heart leads should be *discouraged*. When West sees partner's signal, he will know where the defense must aim.

It isn't always necessary to have a *high* card in partner's suit to encourage him. Suppose you defend 4 ♡ , and partner leads the ♠ A (suggesting possession of the king).

♠ Q 8 5

♠ A led   ■   ♠ 9 2

You may encourage with your 9, since you expect to trump the third round if partner continues.

It is dangerous to discuss signalling situations outside the context of a full deal. In choosing the right signal, you must always consider the defense of the entire deal.

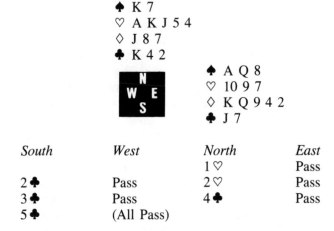

♠ K 7
♡ A K J 5 4
◇ J 8 7
♣ K 4 2

♠ A Q 8
♡ 10 9 7
◇ K Q 9 4 2
♣ J 7

South	West	North	East
		1 ♡	Pass
2 ♣	Pass	2 ♡	Pass
3 ♣	Pass	4 ♣	Pass
5 ♣	(All Pass)		

West leads the ◇ A. **What do you play?**

Good judgment must accompany your signals. Despite your good diamonds, you should play the ◇ 2, asking partner to switch. You hope he will lead a spade through the king. Chances are good that declarer has a singleton diamond and will ruff another diamond lead.

How does partner know that you want a *spade* switch? He must look carefully at dummy and decide what switch is logical. On this deal you couldn't be eager for a heart switch, nor could you be in any hurry to take trump tricks. As it happens, partner switches to the ♠ 3, so you know he has at most five spades. You can cash two spade tricks for sure. Declarer's hand:

♠ J 9 4
♡ Q 6
◇ 5
♣ A Q 10 9 6 5 3

In this deal your ◇ 2 practically *compels* partner to switch because there is an attractive suit for him to switch to (and a danger that declarer will make his game unless the defenders cash out quickly). But a low card may not be so well-defined. It may be noncommittal, it may show doubt, it may show apathy.

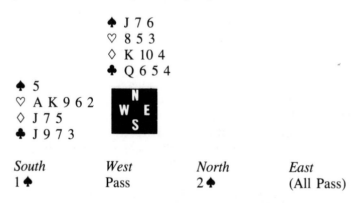

♠ J 7 6
♡ 8 5 3
◇ K 10 4
♣ Q 6 5 4

♠ 5
♡ A K 9 6 2
◇ J 7 5
♣ J 9 7 3

South	West	North	East
1 ♠	Pass	2 ♠	(All Pass)

You lead the ♡A. Partner plays the 7, declarer plays the 4. Although the 7 is partner's lowest, you aren't obliged to switch. For one thing, a switch cannot be desperately needed. (The contract is only two.) Also, no attractive switch is in sight. In this case, partner's play says: "I see no reason to continue hearts." You may do as you like, and we suggest leading the ♡K. Partner could even have a singleton heart(!), and, in any case, another heart lead can't cost.

In contrast, if your hearts are A-K-10-6, you would have to switch. Partner's lowest heart should deny the queen or a doubleton (unless he has the doubleton queen), so a heart continuation may give away a trick.

We said you can show attitude in discarding. Here is an example:

```
              ♠ A 6
              ♡ J 9 3
              ◇ J 4
              ♣ K 9 8 7 6 5
                           ♠ 8 2
          N                ♡ K Q 10 7 2
        W   E              ◇ 10 9 8 7
          S                ♣ 4 3
```

South	West	North	East
1 NT	Pass	3 NT	(All Pass)

West leads the ♠Q, and declarer wins dummy's ace. **What card do you play?** Play the 2, showing no interest in spades. (This is obviously not the time to play high with a doubleton!)

Declarer then leads a club to his ace, a club to the king and a third club from dummy. **What do you discard?**

Discard the ♡10, showing heart strength. Your only chance is for partner to have a club trick plus the ♡A and at least one more

MAKE SURE YOUR DEFENSIVE SIGNALS
ARE CLEAR TO PARTNER.

heart. Even so, you must get him to lead a heart if he gains the lead. It might do to discard your lowest diamond — partner would (or should) conclude that your strength is in hearts. But your lowest diamond is the 7, which may look high to him. Don't take chances — discard the ♡10 even though you are throwing a trick away!

Another trap to avoid: *Declarer, as well as your partner, can see your signals.* Before you signal, consider who can use the information best! Ideally, you would prefer to keep signalling to a minimum and solve your problems by logic only. That isn't always practical, but you must use judgment in deciding whether a signal is really needed.

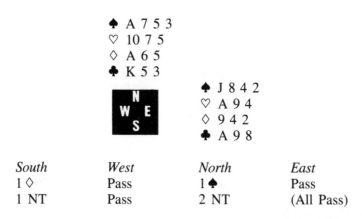

♠ A 7 5 3
♡ 10 7 5
◊ A 6 5
♣ K 5 3

♠ J 8 4 2
♡ A 9 4
◊ 9 4 2
♣ A 9 8

South	West	North	East
1 ◊	Pass	1 ♠	Pass
1 NT	Pass	2 NT	(All Pass)

West leads the ♡2. You win the ace and return the 9. Partner, as it happens, has K-J-6-2, and he cashes three more heart tricks. **What do you discard on the last heart?**

A noncommittal low diamond is best. Don't discard the ♣9. If partner has the ♣QJx, he will switch to clubs without any urging. But if declarer needs a club trick to make his contract (not unlikely, since dummy is weak and you have spades stopped), you will help him if you reveal where the ♣A is. Remember that the purpose of a signal is to suggest a possible course for the defense, not to announce possession of high cards.

Now that you know the most important signal, *attitude*, we can go on to the next-most-important signal . . .

II. *COUNT.* Sometimes the defenders must signal *how many* cards they hold in a suit. Knowing the count may help them decide *when to take a winner* or help them *reconstruct the distribution* of declarer's

hand, an essential task in the defense of most hands. A defender usually signals count when *declarer* leads a suit.

A *high* spot (often followed by a lower one) shows an *even*
number of cards in the suit led.

A *low* spot (often followed by a higher one) suggests an *odd*
number of cards.

Look again at our original problem and see how the defenders
would employ the count signal.

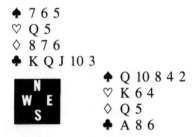

♠ 7 6 5
♡ Q 5
◇ 8 7 6
♣ K Q J 10 3

♠ Q 10 8 4 2
♡ K 6 4
◇ Q 5
♣ A 8 6

West leads the ♡ 10 against South's 3 NT. East covers dummy's
queen with the king, and declarer wins. Declarer then leads a club
toward dummy. Since East wants to win his ♣A at the right time,
he needs to know the count in clubs. West should anticipate partner's problem (if declarer holds the ♣A, West's play doesn't matter) and show count by the way he plays his clubs.

Suppose West follows to the first club with the 2. That could be
a singleton, of course, but then declarer could always stay in touch
with dummy and enjoy his club tricks. East should assume that West
has an *odd* number of clubs — three, to be exact. (West can't have
five clubs, since there are only 13 in the deck.) So declarer has two
clubs, and East therefore *ducks the first club and wins the second.*.

Now say that West plays the 9 on the first club lead. East will
assume that West is showing *two* clubs. (West can't have four clubs,
since declarer wouldn't open 1 NT with a singleton). East would duck
the first *two* club tricks and win the third.

The defenders *must* have a way to signal count in this situation;
otherwise, East must guess when to take his ♣A. Note that the
defenders cannot signal suit length exactly. Usually, however, showing count within a two-card range is good enough to figure out the
exact count. (In the example above, for instance, East knew that

103

declarer had at least two clubs for his 1 NT opening bid. The bidding helps to resolve ambiguous cases.)

Let's talk about *priorities*. When partner inspects your card, how does he know what signal you are using?

In fact, the signals are used with a definite priority. Attitude is the most important signal — it takes precedence. When your partner plays a card you think is a signal, you must first try to interpret his play as attitude. *Interpret his play as count only if his attitude about the suit is known or obvious.*

When declarer voluntarily leads a suit early in the play, he usually has strength in the suit. Attitude therefore is not a concern for the defenders — they shift to giving count if they signal at all.

As you may gather, the defenders do not give count every time declarer leads a suit. The consideration is the same as in showing attitude. You must judge that partner needs the information, and that he, not declarer, can use it better.

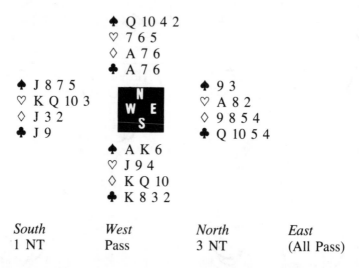

	♠ Q 10 4 2		
	♡ 7 6 5		
	◊ A 7 6		
	♣ A 7 6		

♠ J 8 7 5		♠ 9 3
♡ K Q 10 3		♡ A 8 2
◊ J 3 2		◊ 9 8 5 4
♣ J 9		♣ Q 10 5 4

	♠ A K 6	
	♡ J 9 4	
	◊ K Q 10	
	♣ K 8 3 2	

South	West	North	East
1 NT	Pass	3 NT	(All Pass)

West leads the ♡K. The defenders take four heart tricks and exit safely in a minor suit. Declarer wins in dummy and leads a spade toward his hand. If East is naive enough to play his 9, starting to show an even number of spades, declarer may pick up the spade suit with a fourth-round finesse of the 10 and make his contract. Of course, declarer may guess right regardless, but the defenders shouldn't draw him a road map.

The count signal is usually used as *declarer* leads a suit. You can make an exception in this situation:

♠ Q 7 5
■   ♠ 10 8 4 2

You wind up defending 4 ♡ after partner opened 1 ♠ and you raised to 2 ♠. Partner leads the ♠ A. You may play your ♠ 10. Partner knows you don't have a doubleton spade, since you raised his suit. He should realize that you are showing four cards. However . . .

♢ Q 7 5
■   ♢ J 8 4 2

Declarer opened 1 ♡, partner overcalled 2 ♢, dummy raised to 2 ♡, *you passed,* and declarer jumped to 4 ♡. Partner leads the ♢ A. **What card do you play?** Play the 2, warning against a diamond continuation. Remember, partner will interpret your signal as attitude first. You can't show count because partner cannot know how many diamonds you have. If you play the 8 here, partner will think you have a doubleton and may try to give you a ruff. Try to avoid confusing attitude and count signals. *You can't show count unless your attitude is known or obvious.*

One special case arises in discussing count signals. There is a special way to show count in *trumps.* If a defender played high-low to show two trumps, he might waste a valuable spot with his first play. Therefore, we show count in the trump suit the opposite of count in the side suits.

> Play high-low in trumps to show an odd number.
> Play low-high to show an even number.

Although a count signal in trumps may help you count declarer's distribution, its most frequent purpose is to show or deny the possibility of a *ruff.* Many players, in fact, feel that an *echo* in trumps (a high-low signal, usually showing three) shows definite interest in ruffing.

```
          ♠ 7 5
          ♡ 8 4 2
          ◇ Q J 7 2
          ♣ A K J 6
                              ♠ K Q 2
              ┌─────────┐     ♡ A J 9 5 3
              │    N    │     ◇ A 10 5
              │ W     E │     ♣ 9 3
              │    S    │
              └─────────┘
```

South	West	North	East
			1 ♡
1 ♠	Pass	2 ♣	Pass
2 ♠	Pass	3 ♠	Pass
4 ♠	(All Pass)		

West leads the ♡7. You take the ace and return a heart, declarer winning the king and partner following with the 6. Declarer leads a club to the king and returns a spade from dummy. You play the queen, declarer wins the ace and West plays the 4. Next, declarer leads the ♠J, your partner plays the 3 and you win your king. **What do you lead?**

Lead a third heart and let partner ruff. You know he began with two hearts, and his echo in trumps shows three. Your ◇ A will take the setting trick.

III. SUIT PREFERENCE. This rare and beautiful signal is probably the most overused and abused signal. The most important thing to remember about *suit preference* is that you need it *only in special situations*.

Whereas attitude and count signals are related to their own suit, suit-preference signals direct attention to a suit other than the one in which the signal is given.

> In some cases, you can show strength in a *high-ranking suit* by playing an *unusually high card* in a different suit. You can show strength in a *low-ranking suit* by playing an *unusually low card* in a different suit.

Let's return to our original problem to see how suit preference works.

♠ K 9 6
♡ 8 7
♢ K 4 3 2
♣ K 4 3 2

♠ 3
♡ 5 4 3 2
♢ J 10 9 8
♣ J 10 9 8

You are defending 4 ♡. You lead your singleton spade, and partner wins the ace and returns a spade. You ruff and wonder what to lead next.

This is the most common situation for a suit-preference signal. You need to know where partner's side strength lies. Your partner will anticipate your problem. He will signal, *with the size of the spade he returns for you to ruff,* what suit you should lead next. Suppose partner's hand is:

♠ A 10 7 4 2
♡ 9
♢ Q 7 6 5
♣ A Q 7

He returns the ♠2, his *lowest* spade, asking you to lead clubs, the *lower-ranking* suit, if you ruff. With:

♠ A 10 7 4 2
♡ 9
♢ A Q 7
♣ Q 7 6 5

partner returns the ♠ 10, his *highest,* suggesting strength in diamonds, the *higher-ranking* suit.

Another use of suit preference is to indicate the location of an entry.

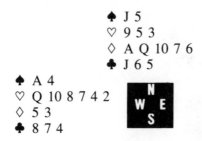

♠ J 5
♡ 9 5 3
◊ A Q 10 7 6
♣ J 6 5

♠ A 4
♡ Q 10 8 7 4 2
◊ 5 3
♣ 8 7 4

You lead the ♡7 against South's notrump contract. Partner puts up the king, ducked, and returns the jack, won by South's ace. **What do you play on this trick?**

If partner gets in, you want him to lead a spade (you know he has no more hearts). But suppose partner's entry is the ◊ K. He won't be sure which black suit to lead. Spades may look risky to him if he has the ♠ Q. But suppose you drop your ♡ Q under declarer's ace. This play costs nothing since all your hearts are good. To follow with a strangely *high* heart carries a message — it shows an entry in the highest-ranking of the other suits. What else could it mean?

Suit preference is often abused. The problems start when players like suit preference so much that they use it where it doesn't belong.

Again, we must establish priorities. Note these principles well.

---

1. *Attitude* first.
2. Interpret a signal as suit preference *only* if no other message is conceivable.
3. A typical suit-preference signal is an *unusual* card with an *unmistakable* significance.

The problems start on a deal like this:

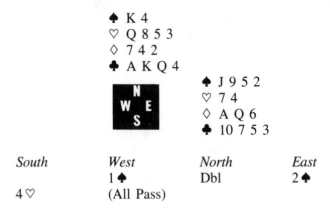

♠ K 4
♡ Q 8 5 3
◇ 7 4 2
♣ A K Q 4

♠ J 9 5 2
♡ 7 4
◇ A Q 6
♣ 10 7 5 3

South	West	North	East
	1♠	Dbl	2♠
4♡	(All Pass)		

West leads the ♠A. **What do you play?**

Remember that your play shows attitude as long as that is a conceivable message. In this case you want partner to *shift* to a diamond, and you can send that message by playing the ♠2. **What does this card say?** You are saying, "Shift!" This is a basic attitude situation, and no fancier signals are needed. Partner looks at dummy and sees that diamonds is the logical suit to shift to.

If you're carried away with suit preference, you may treat East's ♠2 as a request for a shift to clubs, the lower-ranking suit. That is false because:

1. Logically, East cannot want a club shift. And . . .
2. Attitude takes precedence. As long as it is conceivable that East may simply want to ask for a spade continuation or a switch, his signal shows attitude.

Change East's hand to:

♠ J 9 5 2
♡ A 4
◇ 9 5 3
♣ 10 7 5 3

Now what should East play at trick one?

The correct play is the 9 (attitude), asking for *more spades*. There is nothing illogical about a spade continuation, even though dummy can win. A passive defense may be best. Here East can see that West

109

will surely shift to a diamond if East discourages in spades, and a diamond switch may cost the defenders a trick.

Most of the time, the defenders can signal accurately with attitude. Save suit preference for unusual situations.

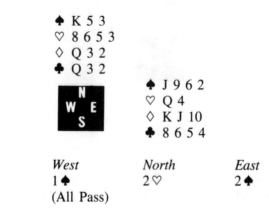

```
              ♠ K 5 3
              ♡ 8 6 5 3
              ◊ Q 3 2
              ♣ Q 3 2
                              ♠ J 9 6 2
                       N      ♡ Q 4
                   W       E  ◊ K J 10
                       S      ♣ 8 6 5 4
```

South	West	North	East
1 ♡	1 ♠	2 ♡	2 ♠
4 ♡	(All Pass)		

West leads the ♣ A. **Which spade do you play as East and why?**

Play the ♠ J, suit preference. First, the ♠ J is an unusually high card when East probably has several cards available. Also, this is a time when suit preference is needed: since the ♠ K is about to give declarer a discard, a switch is needed; but no switch is *obvious* (as it would be if dummy had, say, strong clubs and weak diamonds). The defenders must therefore fall back on suit preference. Attitude won't do the job.

To review:

I. ATTITUDE. The play of a *high* spot is encouraging. The play of a *low* spot is discouraging and may, under some circumstances, demand a switch.

Some important things to remember about ATTITUDE signals:

1. The size of the spot cards is relative. A *4* may encourage if signaller holds A-K-4-3-2; an *8* may discourage if he has 10-9-8. In interpreting a signal, you must look at your own spots, declarer's and dummy's.
2. Decide what message you want to send, then play the *highest* or *lowest* spot you can afford. Avoid signalling with ambiguous spots that may confuse partner.
3. The purpose of a signal is not to announce or deny possession of certain cards, but to suggest a line of defense. Even if you are strong in the suit partner leads, you may signal low if you think it's better for him to lead a different suit.
4. Don't signal if the information may help declarer more than your partner.
5. In discarding, avoid signalling high with a card that may be a vital trick. Instead, discard low in your weaker suits.
6. In signalling from a sequence, play the *top* card, as though you were leading to the trick.
7. Although a high spot is usually a strong signal, a low spot may be ambiguous. It may demand a switch, if an attractive switch is clear; it may also be noncommittal, merely implying doubt or apathy about partner's suit.

II. COUNT. The play of a *high* spot, often followed by a lower one, shows an *even* number of cards. The play of a *low* spot, perhaps followed by a higher one, shows an *odd* number of cards.

Some important things to remember about COUNT signals:

1. The attitude signal takes precedence over count. You may not signal count unless your attitude about a suit is known or obvious.
2. With rare exceptions, defenders use the count signal as *declarer* leads a suit.
3. Signal count only when it is *safe* (declarer, as well as partner, can see your signals!) and when partner *needs* the information.
4. You cannot signal your length exactly, only within a two-card range. In case of ambiguity, the bidding may provide a clue to declarer's exact length.
5. In signalling count, play the *highest* spot you can afford. Avoid ambiguous spots that may confuse partner.
6. To signal count in *trumps*, play *high-low* with an *odd* number. The *trump echo*, as it is called, often implies interest in ruffing.

III. SUIT PREFERENCE. In some cases, you can show strength in a *high-ranking suit* by playing an *unusually high card* in a different suit. You can show strength in a *low-ranking suit* by playing an *unusually low card* in a different suit.

Some important things to remember about SUIT-PREFERENCE signals:

1. The attitude and count signals take precedence over suit preference. Interpret partner's signal as suit preference *only* if he cannot conceivably want to signal attitude or count.
2. A typical suit-preference signal is an *unusual* play with an unmistakable significance.
3. Most of the time, the defenders can handle their signalling problems with attitude. Suit preference is reserved for special situations.
4. The suit-preference signal has many applications. You can indicate the location of an entry, tell partner what suit to lead next after you give him a ruff, or get him to switch to a *specific* suit when an attitude signal would make him guess which suit to switch to.

BE AN ETHICAL PLAYER! The card you play is *itself* a legitimate way to communicate with partner. However, it is unethical to convey information through gestures, remarks or deliberate hesitations. Some players signal encouragement by looking happy or thumping their card on the table when partner leads a suit they like; otherwise they scowl. Avoid these improper methods. Play bridge as a game of skill.

QUIZ ON DEFENSIVE SIGNALS

1.

♠ Q 7 6
♡ A Q 4 2
◊ 4 3 2
♣ 4 3 2

♠ 9 2
♡ J 7 5
◊ J 10 9 8
♣ J 10 9 8

South opened 1 ♡; West overcalled 1 ♠, North raised to 2 ♡ and all passed. West leads the ♠ A. What do you play? Suppose West continues with the ♠ K and ♠ 3, and you ruff. What do you lead?

2.

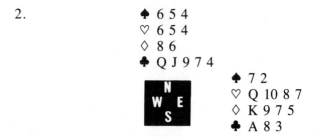

♠ 6 5 4
♡ 6 5 4
◊ 8 6
♣ Q J 9 7 4

♠ 7 2
♡ Q 10 8 7
◊ K 9 7 5
♣ A 8 3

South opened 2 NT, and all passed. West leads the ♠ J. What do you play? Suppose declarer wins the ♠ Q and leads the ♣ K. Partner plays the 6, and you duck. Declarer then continues with the ♣ 10. Partner follows with the 2, and declarer overtakes with dummy's jack. Do you win this trick or duck again?

3.

♠ A K Q 4 3
♡ A 6 5 4
◊ 7 6
♣ 6 5

♠ 8 7
♡ 9 2
◊ A K 8 5 2
♣ A Q 7 2

You opened 1 ◊; North overcalled 1 ♠, East raised you to 2 ◊ and South bid 2 ♡. North raised to 3 ♡, South went on to 4 ♡. You lead ◊ A. Partner plays the 10, declarer plays the 9. What do you lead next?

4.

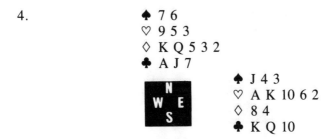

♠ 7 6
♡ 9 5 3
◊ K Q 5 3 2
♣ A J 7

♠ J 4 3
♡ A K 10 6 2
◊ 8 4
♣ K Q 10

You opened 1 ♡. South overcalled 2 ◊, West raised you to 2 ♡, North raised to 3 ◊, passed out. West leads the ♡Q. How do you signal?

5.

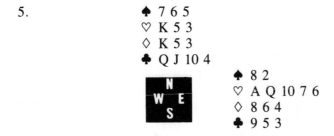

♠ 7 6 5
♡ K 5 3
◊ K 5 3
♣ Q J 10 4

♠ 8 2
♡ A Q 10 7 6
◊ 8 6 4
♣ 9 5 3

South opened 1 NT, North raised to 2 NT, South went on to 3 NT. West leads the ♠J. How do you play to this trick? Declarer wins the ♠Q and leads a low club to the queen. How do you play? Declarer now returns a club from dummy. How do you play?

6.

♠ 9
♡ K 10 4 3
◊ A K Q 8 6
♣ Q 9 4

♠ A K J 5 3
♡ A J 7 2
◊ 7 5 4
♣ 3

You opened 1 ♠; North doubled, East jumped to 3 ♠ (preemptive). South bid 4 ♣, North raised to 5 ♣. You lead the ♠A. Partner plays the 8, and declarer follows with the 4. How do you defend?

7.

    ♠ K J 5 4
    ♡ K J
    ◊ J 8 7 6
    ♣ Q 5 4

        ♠ 7 6
   N   ♡ A Q 10 9
 W **E** ◊ 5 4 3 2
   S   ♣ 8 7 3

South opened 1 NT, North raised to 3 NT. West leads the ♠ 10. Declarer cashes the ♠ A and ♠ Q and leads a spade to dummy. What will you discard on the third and fourth spades?

SOLUTIONS

1. Play the ♠ 9 at trick one (ATTITUDE), asking partner to continue spades, since you want to ruff. Partner's ♠ 3 (SUIT PREFERENCE) asks you to return clubs after taking your ruff.

2. Play the ♠ 2 (ATTITUDE) at trick one. On the second club lead, duck again. Partner's carding shows an even number of clubs (two, in this case), so declarer has another club.

3. Lead the ◊ 2. Partner's encouraging diamond should show the *queen*. (You know, from his raise, that he does not have a doubleton.) Your lead of the ◊ 2 (SUIT PREFERENCE) suggests a club return.

4. Signal with the ♡ 2, suggesting a *switch*. Partner will look at dummy and reason that a club is the most logical switch *from his side of the table*. Note that an attitude signal handles this deal nicely.

5. Play the ♠ 2 at trick one (ATTITUDE), showing a dislike for spades. Play the ♣ 3 at trick two (COUNT), showing an odd number. Play the ♣ 9 at trick three (SUIT PREFERENCE), showing interest in hearts over diamonds.

6. Cash your ♡ A and continue with ♠ K. Partner's ♠ 8 is a routine ATTITUDE signal, asking you to continue spades. As it happens, he has K-6-5-2 of trumps and wants you to force dummy to ruff so his king will win a trick. Remember that a spade continuation is still a possible defense even if dummy can win the next trick.

7. Discard the ◊ 2 and the ♣ 3. By implication, you show interest in the suit you have not discarded. Note that if your diamonds were 10-4-3-2, you couldn't afford to discard one.

Chapter 7

COUNTING

Maybe this sounds like a dull subject, but it is among the most important skills you will learn. No doubt you have seen deals in which declarer locates a missing honor by counting the opponents' high-card points or the distribution of the concealed hands. This is a useful tool, but declarer employs it only occasionally. You won't misplay many dummies even if you forget to count the opponents' points and distribution.

But if you don't make a *habit* of counting on defense, you're in for trouble. *Producing consistently good defense will be impossible.*

Counting on defense has several applications. In Chapter 1, you saw that the defenders can benefit from counting their *tricks,* just as declarer routinely counts his winners and losers. The other aspects of defensive counting are just as important.

---

1. COUNT DECLARER'S DISTRIBUTION. The bidding may give you a rough idea of declarer's distribution. If declarer opens or rebids in notrump, for example, his pattern will be balanced: 4-3-3-3, 4-4-3-2, or 5-3-3-2. If declarer opens 1 ♢, rebids 2 ♣ and then bids diamonds again, you can expect six diamonds and four clubs. You can also use information from partner's opening lead and distributional signals, and from watching as players fail to follow suit. Soon you may have a complete count.

2. COUNT DECLARER'S HIGH-CARD POINTS. The bidding may tell you approximately how many points declarer has (such as when he opens 1 NT). As the play proceeds, you can see what cards constitute declarer's high-card strength (and therefore what honors your partner has).

3. COUNT DECLARER'S TRICKS. A count of declarer's possible tricks tells you whether you must adopt an active or passive defensive strategy.

Our goal is for you to realize the importance of counting on every hand you defend. True, you must keep many things in mind during the defense, but counting is the most worthwhile.

I. DECLARER'S DISTRIBUTION

1.
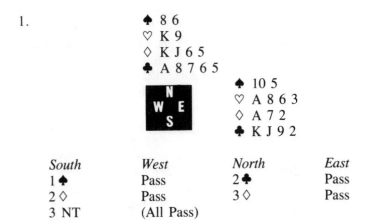

```
              ♠ 8 6
              ♡ K 9
              ◇ K J 6 5
              ♣ A 8 7 6 5
                              ♠ 10 5
                              ♡ A 8 6 3
                              ◇ A 7 2
                              ♣ K J 9 2
```

South	West	North	East
1 ♠	Pass	2 ♣	Pass
2 ◇	Pass	3 ◇	Pass
3 NT	(All Pass)		

West leads the ♡2. Dummy plays low, and you win the ace. **How do you defend?**

Let's see what you can deduce about declarer's hand. He has some spades and diamonds. **How many does he have of each?** More spades, surely. He would open 1 ◇ with four spades and four diamonds. **Does declarer have a six-card spade suit?** Not likely, since he bid spades only once. **Does he have five spades and five diamonds?** Again, unlikely. With that distribution, he would prefer to play game in diamonds. Declarer should have *five spades and four diamonds.* **Now, how many hearts does he have?** From partner's opening lead of the ♡2, declarer has three hearts. **How many clubs does he have?** One at most. **How do you defend?** Shift to a club — the *king,* in case declarer's club is the queen.

2.

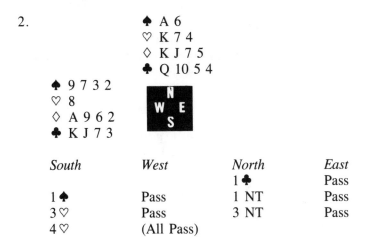

South	West	North	East
		1 ♣	Pass
1 ♠	Pass	1 NT	Pass
3 ♡	Pass	3 NT	Pass
4 ♡	(All Pass)		

You lead the ◊ A, winning the first trick. **What do you lead next?** Declarer has shown at least ten major-suit cards, so he has at most three cards in the minors. Suppose he has two low clubs. In that case, you must lead a club right away. Declarer is now void in diamonds and can discard a club on the ◊ K. **Can a club lead cost if declarer's clubs are A-x?** No, he could discard his low club on the ◊ K anyway. So a club lead at trick two is mandatory.

3.

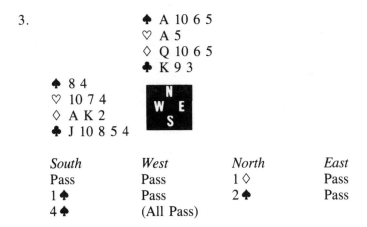

South	West	North	East
Pass	Pass	1 ◊	Pass
1 ♠	Pass	2 ♠	Pass
4 ♠	(All Pass)		

You lead the ♣ J (better than cashing a winner in dummy's long suit). The jack wins the first trick, but declarer ruffs the next club. He leads a trump to the ace and a trump back to his king, partner following. Next, declarer cashes the ♡ A and follows with the ♡ K and ♡ Q. He leads a fourth heart, ruffing in dummy as partner follows

119

with the jack. Declarer then ruffs dummy's last club and leads a diamond toward dummy. **What do you play?**

You know declarer has one club, four hearts and no more than five spades. He therefore has at least three diamonds. You should play your 2. If declarer has three low diamonds, he will probably try the 10 from dummy (his best percentage play), losing to partner's jack.

Note that you must do your counting *in advance* — when declarer leads a diamond, you can play low without a revealing pause.

4.

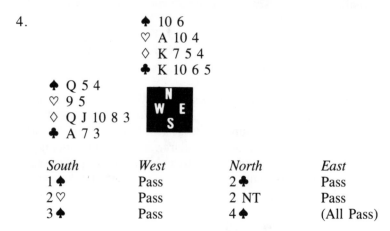

	♠ 10 6		
	♡ A 10 4		
	◊ K 7 5 4		
	♣ K 10 6 5		

♠ Q 5 4
♡ 9 5
◊ Q J 10 8 3
♣ A 7 3

South	West	North	East
1 ♠	Pass	2 ♣	Pass
2 ♡	Pass	2 NT	Pass
3 ♠	Pass	4 ♠	(All Pass)

You lead the ◊ Q. Declarer wins the king in dummy and finesses the ♠ 10 to your queen. You continue diamonds, and declarer wins the ace. His next play is the ♣ J. **Do you win the ace or duck?**

Clearly, you should win. Declarer's bidding promises six or more spades (probably only six this time, since he took a finesse in the suit) and four hearts. He has followed to two diamonds, so the ♣ J must be a singleton.

LET'S SEE NOW - DECLARER HAS 4♠, AND FROM THE LOOKS OF PARD'S LEAD, 3♢S. THAT'S 6 CARDS LEFT IN ♣S AND ♡S. 6 SPLITS 4-2 A LOT OF THE TIME. DOES WEST HAVE 4♡? NO. HE WOULD HAVE BID 1♡ OVER 1♢, NOT 1♠. SO, GIVE HIM 2♡S AND 4♣S. I HAVE 3♡, DUMMY HAS 4, SO GIVE PARD 4 ♡S. PARD HAS 3♣S, AND IT LOOKS LIKE 4♢S. SO, SHE HAS 2♣S. WAIT. THAT ADDS UP TO ONLY 12♣S. SHE MUST HAVE 3♣S. SO 3-3 IN CLUBS AND ♡S. DECLARER IS 4-3-3-3 SO IS PA... NOW LE... COUNT... POINTS...

5.

North:
♠ A 8 5 3
♡ J 10 7
♢ Q 6
♣ K J 6 5

East:
♠ Q 10 9 4
♡ Q 6 4 2
♢ A 2
♣ 9 7 3

South	West	North	East
1 ♣	Pass	1 ♠	Pass
2 ♠	Pass	3 ♣	Pass
3 NT	(All Pass)		

West leads the ♢4. Dummy plays low, and you win your ace. **How do you defend?**

By this time, we hope you won't return your partner's suit first and think later. Partner's ♢4 lead tells you he had at most a five-card suit, so declarer has *four diamonds*. But declarer opened 1♣, so he has at least *four clubs*. Declarer raised North's 1♠ response, suggesting at least *three spades*. (Actually, declarer should have *four* spades to raise, but that would mean he bid notrump with a singleton heart, which is impossible.) So you conclude that declarer's distribution is 3-2-4-4.

Declarer figures to have at least one diamond honor, since West would have led the jack from K-J-10-x-x, and declarer may have two honors. Declarer is therefore sure to have a diamond stopper. Since you know declarer has only two hearts, a heart shift is best. The missing cards:

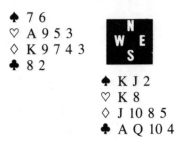

♠ 7 6
♡ A 9 5 3
◊ K 9 7 4 3
♣ 8 2

♠ K J 2
♡ K 8
◊ J 10 8 5
♣ A Q 10 4

Your ♡2 lead goes to partner's ace. You duck the heart return, and declarer must win the king. When declarer leads a diamond, West wins and returns a heart, giving the defenders five tricks. See what happens if you neglect to count and thoughtlessly return your partner's lead?

II. DECLARER'S HIGH-CARD POINTS

6.

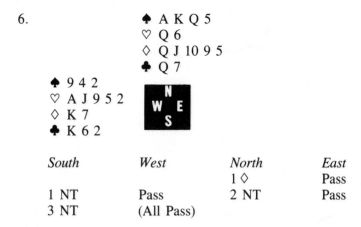

♠ A K Q 5
♡ Q 6
◊ Q J 10 9 5
♣ Q 7

♠ 9 4 2
♡ A J 9 5 2
◊ K 7
♣ K 6 2

South	West	North	East
		1 ◊	Pass
1 NT	Pass	2 NT	Pass
3 NT	(All Pass)		

You lead the ♡5, and dummy's queen wins the first trick. At trick two declarer leads the ◇Q to your king. **What do you lead now?**

You know declarer has the ♡K (and no more than three hearts, since he responded 1 NT to the opening bid). It looks as if he has the ◇A and has taken a losing finesse. But if declarer holds the ♡K and ◇A, he cannot have the ♣A. You can lead a club to partner's ace, and the heart return will set this contract a lot! (The contract is still defeated even if declarer has the ♣A. Then partner will have the ◇A, and declarer cannot take nine tricks without diamond tricks.)

7.

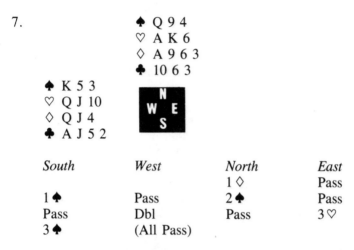

```
              ♠ Q 9 4
              ♡ A K 6
              ◇ A 9 6 3
              ♣ 10 6 3
 ♠ K 5 3
 ♡ Q J 10          N
 ◇ Q J 4        W     E
 ♣ A J 5 2         S
```

South	West	North	East
		1 ◇	Pass
1 ♠	Pass	2 ♠	Pass
Pass	Dbl	Pass	3 ♡
3 ♠	(All Pass)		

You lead the ♡Q. Dummy wins, and declarer passes the ♠9 to your king. You continue a heart to dummy. Declarer draws trumps with the queen and ace, and partner discards on the third round. Declarer then cashes the ◇K, leads a diamond toward dummy and ducks your jack. **How do you defend?**

Declarer has ♠AJxxx and the ◇K. Does he have the ♣K too? No, then he would have been interested in game with his 11 HCP; he would have bid over the raise to 2 ♠. You can lead a club to partner's king, and the club return will trap the queen (if declarer has it). Depending on what spot partner returns, you will know whether you can cash three club tricks or two clubs and a heart.

8.

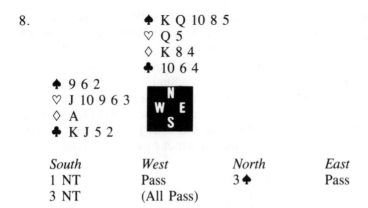

♠ K Q 10 8 5
♡ Q 5
◊ K 8 4
♣ 10 6 4

♠ 9 6 2
♡ J 10 9 6 3
◊ A
♣ K J 5 2

South	West	North	East
1 NT	Pass	3 ♠	Pass
3 NT	(All Pass)		

You lead the ♡J. Declarer plays dummy's queen, winning the first trick. He then leads a diamond to his queen and your ace. **What do you lead now?**

Declarer has 16 to 18 HCP for his opening. He surely has the ♡A and ♡K. East would have played either of those cards if he could. Declarer also has the ◊Q — you saw him play it. What does declarer have in spades? He probably has the ace. If he did not, his first lead would be a spade to establish his best suit. (You just drew an *inference* from the way declarer is playing the hand. We will study this subject more later.)

Assuming that declarer has the ♠A, you know 13 of his high-card points. **Therefore, how good are his clubs?** They can't be as good as A-Q. That would give him 19 HCP, too many for his bid. Since partner must hold a club honor, a club shift can't cost and may be the only way to beat the contract. The missing cards:

♠ 7 4 3
♡ 8 7
◊ J 10 7 3 2
♣ A 9 8

♠ A J
♡ A K 4 2
◊ Q 9 6 5
♣ Q 7 3

This deal has another important point. You assumed that declarer had the ♠A, so he had five tricks available there. You knew he had three heart winners, plus an established ◊K in dummy. So he had *nine tricks ready to cash.* A club shift, hoping for four fast tricks, was your only chance. If declarer held the ♣A, he would inevitably make the contract with overtricks. But if East had the ace, a club shift was vital before declarer took his nine tricks.

III. DECLARER'S TRICKS

9.
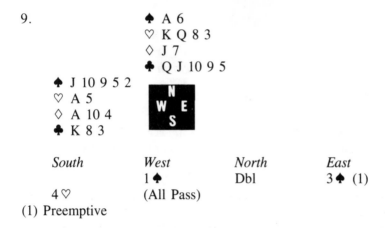

	♠ A 6		
	♡ K Q 8 3		
	◊ J 7		
	♣ Q J 10 9 5		

♠ J 10 9 5 2
♡ A 5
◊ A 10 4
♣ K 8 3

South	West	North	East
	1 ♠	Dbl	3 ♠ (1)
4 ♡	(All Pass)		

(1) Preemptive

You lead the ♠J. Dummy wins, and declarer drops the queen. The ♡K is led from dummy. You win and lead another spade, declarer ruffing. He draws another round of trumps (partner follows) and passes the ♣Q to your king. **What do you lead?**

Counting declarer's tricks will help. He has no more than four in hearts, one in spades and four in clubs. Thus, he can't make the contract without a diamond trick. *Don't* panic and cash the ◊A. Just exit with a club and wait for declarer to lead diamonds himself.

Another way of looking at it is that declarer has one spade and at most five hearts, and therefore seven or more minor-suit cards. After he finishes taking his club tricks, he will still have two diamonds left. If you have two diamond tricks coming, you'll get them.

10.

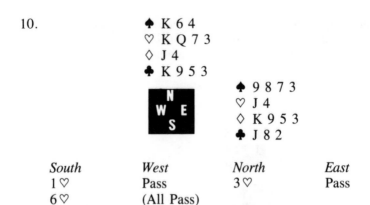

♠ K 6 4
♡ K Q 7 3
◇ J 4
♣ K 9 5 3

♠ 9 8 7 3
♡ J 4
◇ K 9 5 3
♣ J 8 2

South	West	North	East
1 ♡	Pass	3 ♡	Pass
6 ♡	(All Pass)		

West leads the ♠ Q. Declarer wins the ace, leads to the ♠ K and ruffs a spade high. He draws two rounds of trumps (your partner follows), cashes the ◇ A and exits with a diamond to your king. **What do you lead?**

How many tricks does declarer have? Five hearts and two spades, plus the ◇ A and the ♣ A and ♣ K. That's ten tricks. If he has two diamonds left, he can take 12 tricks by ruffing them in dummy. Declarer will also make the contract if he has the ♣ Q. The correct return is a diamond. If declarer has a diamond left, he will ruff this trick in dummy, which he intends to do anyway. Even if declarer is out of diamonds and you give up a ruff-and-discard, that will be only 11 tricks. Declarer can't take another if he lacks the ♣ Q.

Breaking the clubs for declarer is dangerous, and a spade return would give declarer a ruff-and-discard he *could* use if his pattern were 2-5-3-3 — he could ruff in dummy and discard his club loser.

Here are the types of counting on defense.

| COUNT DECLARER'S DISTRIBUTION |
| COUNT DECLARER'S HIGH-CARD POINTS |
| COUNT DECLARER'S TRICKS |

Form the habit of counting declarer's distribution and high-card points on *every* hand you defend. Count his tricks if you need to. Remember the importance of counting in producing good defense.

QUIZ ON COUNTING ON DEFENSE

1.
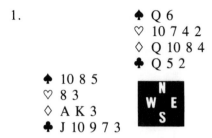

                   ♠ Q 6
                   ♡ 10 7 4 2
                   ◊ Q 10 8 4
                   ♣ Q 5 2

♠ 10 8 5
♡ 8 3
◊ A K 3
♣ J 10 9 7 3

South opened 1 ♡ and went to 4 ♡ after North raised to 2 ♡. You lead the ♣J, which holds. Declarer ruffs the next club and draws two rounds of trumps, your partner's jack falling on the second round. Next, declarer leads the ♠Q, a spade to his king and the ♠A. He ruffs a fourth round of spades in dummy, as partner plays the jack, and ruffs a club back to his hand. Declarer then leads a low diamond toward dummy. How do you defend?

2.
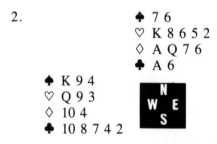

                   ♠ 7 6
                   ♡ K 8 6 5 2
                   ◊ A Q 7 6
                   ♣ A 6

♠ K 9 4
♡ Q 9 3
◊ 10 4
♣ 10 8 7 4 2

South opened 1 ◊, North responded 1 ♡; South rebid 1 ♠, North jumped to 3 ◊. South bid 3 NT. You lead the ♣4. Dummy plays the 6, and partner wins the king and returns the ♣3, declarer following low to both tricks. At trick three declarer leads a spade to his queen, and you win the king. How do you defend?

3.
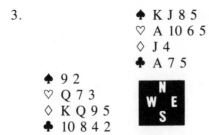

♠ K J 8 5
♡ A 10 6 5
◊ J 4
♣ A 7 5

♠ 9 2
♡ Q 7 3
◊ K Q 9 5
♣ 10 8 4 2

South opened 1♠, North raised to 3♠, South bid 6♠. You lead the ◊K. Declarer wins the ace and draws two rounds of trumps, your partner following. Next, declarer plays the ♣K and ♣A and ruffs a club in his hand. Declarer then exits with a diamond to your queen. How do you defend?

4.

♠ A 5
♡ 8 6 5
◊ K J 6 2
♣ A 10 9 4

♠ K 9 3
♡ A Q 10 7 3
◊ 8 7
♣ K J 5

You, East, opened 1♡. South overcalled 2◊, North raised to 4◊, South went on to 5◊. Partner leads the ♡ 2. You win the ace, and declarer drops the king. Declarer ruffs the next heart and draws two rounds of trumps, your partner following once. South ruffs dummy's last heart and leads the ♣Q from his hand, ducking in dummy. You win the ♣K. How do you defend?

5.
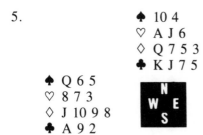
♠ 10 4
♡ A J 6
◊ Q 7 5 3
♣ K J 7 5

♠ Q 6 5
♡ 8 7 3
◊ J 10 9 8
♣ A 9 2

South opened 1♠, North responded 2♣; South rebid 2♡, North bid 2 NT; South tried 3♠, North raised to 4♠. You lead the ◊ J. Declarer wins the ace, plays off the A-K of trumps and leads another trump to your queen. Partner follows with the jack on the second trump and discards on the third. Declarer ruffs your diamond continuation and leads a club from his hand. Do you win or duck?

6.

♠ A Q J 10 4
♡ K 7 6
◊ J 5
♣ 10 6 5

♠ 9 7
♡ A J
◊ Q 10 8 7 4
♣ K J 4 2

North opened 1♠, South responded 2 NT, North raised to 3 NT. You lead the ◊ 7, won by dummy's jack. Declarer then leads a heart to his queen. How do you defend?

7.

♠ Q 9 6 4
♡ Q 7 5
◊ A J 9 3
♣ J 3

♠ A 5
♡ 8 6 4 2
◊ K Q 4 2
♣ Q 10 7

South opened 1 ♠, North responded 2 ◊; South rebid 2 ♠, North raised to 3 ♠, South went on to 4 ♠. West leads the ♡ J. Declarer wins in his hand with the ♡ K and leads a trump to the queen and your ace. You return a heart to dummy's queen. Declarer draws another round of trumps, your partner following, cashes the ♡ A and leads the ◊ 10, passing it to your queen. How do you defend?

8.

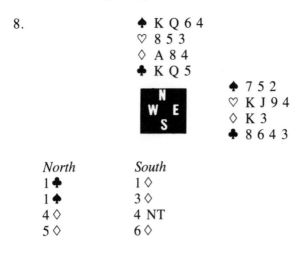

♠ K Q 6 4
♡ 8 5 3
◊ A 8 4
♣ K Q 5

♠ 7 5 2
♡ K J 9 4
◊ K 3
♣ 8 6 4 3

North	South
1 ♣	1 ◊
1 ♠	3 ◊
4 ◊	4 NT
5 ◊	6 ◊

West leads the ♡ 2. You play the jack (you know declarer holds the ace), and declarer wins the queen. He leads the ◊ Q and finesses to your king. How do you defend?

SOLUTIONS

1. Play a low diamond. Declarer is known to have five hearts, four spades and one club, so he has three diamonds. If he lacks the ◊J, he will probably finesse the ◊10. Note that you must do your counting in advance so you can play low without pause.
2. Declarer is marked with four clubs from partner's plays. (Partner would win the ♣Q with K-Q-3 and would return the ♣J with K-J-3.) Declarer bid spades and diamonds and should have four cards in each suit; so he has at most a singleton heart. Shift to the ♡Q, in case declarer's singleton is the jack.
3. Declarer had five spades and two clubs. If he had three diamonds and three hearts, you can get out safely with a *diamond*. A diamond return is also safe if declarer had two diamonds and four hearts — a ruff-and-discard won't help him. A heart return runs an obvious risk, and a club return would give declarer a ruff-and-discard he *could* use if he had three diamonds and three hearts.
4. Count declarer's tricks. He has six diamonds and one spade. Even if you return a club and give him three club tricks, he is still a trick short and must lose a spade to you eventually. Any other return costs the contract, since declarer's hand is:

> ♠ Q x x x
> ♡ K
> ◊ A Q 10 x x x
> ♣ Q x

5. Play low, since declarer's pattern should be 6-4-1-2.
6. Declarer's 2 NT response promised 13-15 HCP. He has the ◊A and ◊K and the ♡Q, and surely holds the ♠K — if he lacked that card, he would lead spades, not hearts, to set up his best suit. So declarer lacks the ♣A, and a club shift and return may net five tricks for the defense.

7. This is similar to hand #4. Declarer is known to have four spade tricks and three hearts. A diamond return will give him two tricks in diamonds, but he will still be a trick short unless he has the ♣A. A club return gives him a chance to make a hopeless contract if his hand is:

> ♠ K J 10 x x
> ♡ A K x
> ◇ 10 x
> ♣ K x x

(Declarer cannot hold ◇ 10xx and the doubleton ♣A; he would lead the ♣A and a club for a sure endplay.)

8. Declarer has at most six diamond tricks and two hearts. He can't make the contract if he lacks the ♠A (unless he happens to be void in spades), but he might make it without the ♣A, unless you lead a club. If declarer had four spade tricks, that would get him up to 12. Declarer's hand:

> ♠ A J x
> ♡ A Q
> ◇ Q J 10 x x x x
> ♣ x

Chapter 8

DEFENDERS' CARD COMBINATIONS;
INFERRING CARD COMBINATIONS

The ability to visualize how the cards in a suit lie around the table and what will happen when the suit is led is the essence of a quality called *card sense*. Although this quality is hard to define, all good card players have it. Developing card sense is important — especially on defense, where you can't see your partner's or declarer's cards. Luckily, card sense can be acquired — that is what this chapter will help you do.

First, let's look at situations in which the defenders must handle a card combination correctly. Then we'll see how the defenders can *infer* declarer's holding from the way he plays a suit.

I. DEFENDERS' CARD COMBINATIONS

1. *Unblocking:*

The defenders may have trouble cashing tricks because of a *blocked suit.* Overcoming a blockage requires foresight and concentration as well as technical knowledge.

$$\heartsuit\ 10$$
$$\heartsuit\ A\,J\,7\,5\,3 \qquad \blacksquare \qquad \heartsuit\ K\,8\,6\,2$$
$$\heartsuit\ Q\,9\,4$$

West leads the $\heartsuit$ 5 against a notrump contract. East wins the king and returns the 2 to West's jack. West then cashes the ace. East must be careful to throw his *8,* unblocking, so the defense can take all five tricks.

$$\heartsuit\ A$$
$$\heartsuit\ Q\,9\,8\,7\,2 \qquad \blacksquare \qquad \heartsuit\ K\,J\,3$$
$$\heartsuit\ 10\,6\,5\,4$$

West leads the $\heartsuit$ 7 against notrump, and dummy's ace wins. East must unblock the jack to let the defenders take their tricks. How does East know to throw his jack? He can apply the *Rule of Eleven,* which reveals that declarer has only one card higher than West's 7. No matter what that card is, East loses nothing by parting with the jack.

$$\heartsuit\ Q\,5$$
$$\heartsuit\ A\,10\,8\,6\,4\,2 \qquad \blacksquare \qquad \heartsuit\ J\,9$$
$$\heartsuit\ K\,7\,3$$

West leads the $\heartsuit$ 6 against notrump, and dummy's queen wins. East must unblock his jack to untangle the defenders' suit. (East can infer that declarer lacks the 10, else declarer would duck the lead to his hand.)

$$\heartsuit\ Q\,4$$
$$\heartsuit\ A\,9\,8\,6\,2 \qquad \blacksquare \qquad \heartsuit\ J\,10\,5$$
$$\heartsuit\ K\,7\,3$$

West leads the $\heartsuit$ 6 against notrump, and dummy's queen wins. East must unblock the jack.

2. *Surrounding Plays:*

Suppose you are East, needing fast heart tricks in this position:

♡ 10 8 5
■   ♡ K J 9 2

You must hope partner has the ace, of course, but he won't need the queen as well — provided you are careful to *lead your jack*. The suit may be:

♡ 10 8 5
♡ A 7 4   ■   ♡ K J 9 2
♡ Q 6 3

Declarer is helpless if you lead the jack. If you lead low, he can duck, forcing your partner to win the ace and saving a stopper with the queen behind your king.

The same situation from the other side of the table:

♡ Q 6 3
♡ K J 9 2   ■   ♡ A 7 4
♡ 10 8 5

If you must attack this suit as West, lead the *jack*. If you were desperate, you would lead the jack even without the crucial 9 to back it up. The situation could be:

♡ Q 6 3
♡ K J 8   ■   ♡ A 9 4 2
♡ 10 7 5

or even:

♡ Q 6 3
♡ K J 2   ■   ♡ A 9 8 4
♡ 10 7 5

All of the variations on this *surrounding* theme have the same premise. You may gain by *leading as though you had a sequential holding*.

$\heartsuit$ 9 6 4

$\heartsuit$ K 7 2 ■ $\heartsuit$ Q 10 8 5

$\heartsuit$ A J 3

East, who must lead this suit, begins with the *10,* the card he would have led if he held the 9.

$\heartsuit$ A J 5

$\heartsuit$ K 10 8 4 ■ $\heartsuit$ Q 7 2

$\heartsuit$ 9 6 3

If West must break this suit, he should lead the 10.

$\heartsuit$ A Q 4

$\heartsuit$ K J 9 ■ $\heartsuit$ 8 7 6 5

$\heartsuit$ 10 3 2

If West is obliged to break this suit, he prevents declarer from winning three tricks by leading the jack.

3. *Communication:*

You studied situations in which the defenders must preserve their own communication or disrupt declarer's.

$\heartsuit$ 6 5 4

$\heartsuit$ Q J 10 8 3 ■ $\heartsuit$ K 7

$\heartsuit$ A 9 2

West leads the $\heartsuit$ Q against notrump. East must overtake with the king to get out of his partner's way. If East plays low, declarer can win the first trick and block the suit.
Less obvious is:

$\heartsuit$ K 6 5 2

$\heartsuit$ Q J 10 8 4 ■ $\heartsuit$ A 7

$\heartsuit$ 9 3

West leads the $\heartsuit$ Q against notrump. Regardless of what dummy plays, East must get his *ace* out of the way and return the 7, establishing West's suit.

♡ K 6 5

♡ J 10 9 4 2 ■ ♡ Q 7

♡ A 8 3

West leads the ♡J against notrump. East should play his queen (even if dummy's king wins). This play locates the queen for West and unblocks the suit.(If East plays low, declarer lets the queen win on the second heart lead, and East can't lead the suit again.)

♡ 8 6 4

♡ K Q 10 7 2 ■ ♡ A 5

♡ J 9 3

West leads the ♡K against notrump. (Many of the plays we are discussing are also winners at a suit contract.) East must *overtake with the ace* and return the suit to unblock.

The lead of the queen from A-Q-J-x-x against notrump is intended to force out declarer's king while maintaining communication with partner. Here is a similar situation.

♡ K 7 5

♡ A Q 10 6 4 ■ ♡ 8 2

♡ J 9 3

If you must attack this suit, you do best to lead the *queen*. If declarer plays dummy's king, you keep communication open while retaining your A-10 as a *tenace* behind declarer's jack. Maybe this is better classified as a surrounding play.

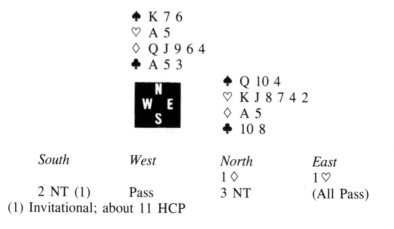

♠ K 7 6
♡ A 5
◇ Q J 9 6 4
♣ A 5 3

♠ Q 10 4
♡ K J 8 7 4 2
◇ A 5
♣ 10 8

South	West	North	East
		1 ◇	1 ♡
2 NT (1)	Pass	3 NT	(All Pass)

(1) Invitational; about 11 HCP

West leads the ♡9, and dummy plays low. **How do you defend?**

Your partner probably led from a doubleton heart, and declarer has Q-10-x. (Partner might have led another suit with only one heart.) Since declarer will always take two heart tricks, you can afford to duck the first trick, signalling encouragement with the 8. The advantage is that you let declarer win one of his heart tricks while your partner still has a heart to lead. (Unless partner has one trick to contribute, the contract is unbeatable.) The missing hands may be:

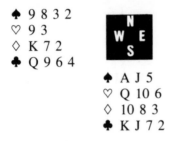

♠ 9 8 3 2
♡ 9 3
◊ K 7 2
♣ Q 9 6 4

♠ A J 5
♡ Q 10 6
◊ 10 8 3
♣ K J 7 2

Declarer wins the ♡10 and leads a diamond. West wins and leads his other heart, establishing your suit while you have the ◊ A for an entry. Note the outcome if you win the ♡K at trick one and return a heart. Your communication is gone.

4. *Entries:*

We mentioned the defenders' entry problems when we discussed defense against notrump. The following situation is unusual:

♡ 5

♡ A 9 8 3 2 ■ ♡ K 10 4

♡ Q J 7 6

West leads the ♡3 vs. notrump. East wins the king and returns the 10, covered by declarer's jack. If West lacks a side entry, he should duck, preserving his A-9 behind declarer and keeping communication. (Assuming that West has no side entry, declarer could limit the defense to three heart tricks by playing low on the second heart.)

ENTRIES!
ENTRIES
HEERE!

♠ A Q 10 7 5
♡ A J
◇ 7 5 3
♣ A Q 8

♠ K J 8
♡ K 8 5 3
◇ Q 10
♣ J 9 5 2

South	West	North	East
		1 ♠	Pass
1 NT	Pass	2 NT	(All Pass)

West leads the ◇ 6. Declarer ducks your queen but wins the second diamond with the ace. Next, declarer passes the ♠9 to your jack. **How do you defend?**

To beat the contract, you must get your partner in to cash his diamond tricks. Partner's only possible entry is the ♡ Q, so you *lead the ♡ K,* drilling an entry to his hand. To lead low wouldn't be good enough.

Overtaking partner's winner is routine if you see that he can't want to remain on lead:

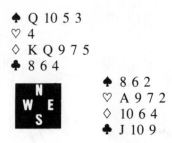

♠ Q 10 5 3
♥ 4
♦ K Q 9 7 5
♣ 8 6 4

♠ 8 6 2
♥ A 9 7 2
♦ 10 6 4
♣ J 10 9

West, having overcalled in hearts, leads the ♥K against declarer's 4♠ contract. East should overtake with the ace and shift to the ♣J.

Some defensive card combinations force you to depart from the usual way of leading to a trick.

♠ K 7 5

♠ 9 4
♠ A Q J 2

♠ 10 8 6 3

Defending against notrump, East must attack this suit. He should lead *low*, saving his honors behind dummy's K-x-x. Since declarer has 10-x-x-x, leading an honor will cost East a trick.

♠ 8 7 5

♠ A 9
♠ K Q 10 4

♠ J 6 3 2

The defenders need to cash three fast tricks in this suit. East, on lead, must play West for the ace, so he may as well lead *low*. When declarer plays low, West must win the *ace* and return the 9.

In the last two examples, it was correct to lead low from a sequential holding. It can also be right to lead an honor (from length) without a sequence.

♥ 10 5

♥ A Q 7 4
♥ J 9 3

♥ K 8 6 2

The defenders must cash three fast heart tricks in this position. East therefore leads the jack.

140

◇ A 10 8

◇ J 9 2   ■   ◇ Q 7 6 5

◇ K 4 3

West is endplayed and is forced to lead this suit. He should lead the jack. If West leads low, dummy's 8 forces East's queen, and declarer then finesses against West's jack.

◇ Q 10

◇ K J 7 3   ■   ◇ A 8 4

◇ 9 6 5 2

West attacks this suit by leading the king. East unblocks the 8. West then leads a diamond to the ace, and the diamond return goes through declarer's 9-6 to West's J-7. If West leads low on the first round (or East fails to unblock), the defenders can't take four fast tricks.

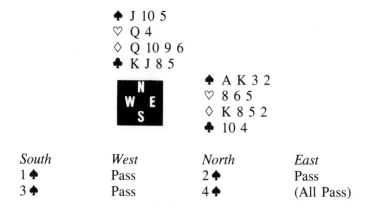

♠ J 10 5
♡ Q 4
◇ Q 10 9 6
♣ K J 8 5

♠ A K 3 2
♡ 8 6 5
◇ K 8 5 2
♣ 10 4

South	West	North	East
1 ♠	Pass	2 ♠	Pass
3 ♠	Pass	4 ♠	(All Pass)

West leads the ♡J, won by dummy's queen. Declarer leads the ♠J from dummy, you duck, and the jack wins, West following low. You win the king on the next spade lead, and partner discards a low club. **How do you defend?**

You appear to have no heart or club tricks, so you must try for two diamonds, or one diamond plus an extra trump trick. Assume declarer has a singleton diamond, since he will always be down if he has two. Can you beat the contract if declarer has only one diamond? Yes, a forcing defense will work. Declarer has only one more trump than you at this stage, and you still have the trump ace. If you can force him to ruff twice, you gain control.

Suppose you lead a low diamond. Not good enough. Partner wins, but declarer ruffs your king on the diamond return. He can win the next diamond with dummy's queen instead of ruffing. But suppose you lead your ♢K, then a low diamond. Declarer is helpless. If he discards, West takes the setting trick with the ♢A. If declarer ruffs, you can force out his last trump with another diamond lead when you win your ace of trumps.

II. INFERRING CARD COMBINATIONS

Assuming you can trust declarer to play *his* card combinations logically, you can draw conclusions about his holding. This will help you reconstruct declarer's high cards, distribution and possible tricks.

Suppose you defend a 4♠ contract. Declarer has drawn trumps, leaving some trumps still in dummy, and now he is ready to lead hearts. Dummy has K-J-9-3, you sit in front of dummy with A-8-4. Declarer leads low toward dummy. You duck, and declarer plays the 9, losing to partner's 10. **What conclusions can you draw?**

Your partner surely has the ♡Q. Also, declarer has at least two more hearts. If he had only a doubleton heart, he would play the ♡K or ♡J from dummy, hoping for only one heart loser. Thus, when declarer leads a second heart toward dummy, you should *duck again*. Declarer will have a chance to guess wrong again (by playing dummy's jack).

Here are other examples. In each one, the contract is 4♠, trumps remain in dummy and declarer leads hearts.

♡ K 10 9 4

♡ A 7 3 ■

Declarer leads low to the 9, losing to partner's jack. **Can declarer have Q-x?** No. He could hold his losers to one with that holding. **Can he have x-x?** No. He would put up dummy's ♡K, hoping for only one loser in the suit. **Can he have x-x-x or Q-x-x-(x)?** Yes.

♡ 5 3

♡ Q J 4 2 ■

Declarer leads low from dummy and plays the 10 from his hand, losing to your jack. **Can declarer have x-x-x?** No, partner would win the trick if he had both the ace and king. **Can declarer have K-10-x?** No, he would put up his king, hoping for only one heart loser. **Can declarer have A-10-x-(x)?** Yes.

142

♡ Q J 10 3

♡ K 9 6 4

Declarer leads low toward dummy. **Can he have A-x-(x)?** Unlikely, since he would have a chance for no losers by taking a finesse. (However, declarer might play deceptively if he suspects you have the king.) Partner probably has the ace.

♡ K 4

■ ♡ A Q 8 5

Partner leads the ♡ 3 to trick one, and declarer puts up dummy's king. **Can declarer have J-x-(x)?** No, he would *duck* the first trick in dummy if he held the jack, hoping partner had led from the queen. Partner has the jack.

♡ 10 5 3

♡ K Q 9 4 ■

Your lead of the ♡ K holds the first trick. **Declarer may have the ace, but does he also have the jack?** No, with A-J he could assure a second trick by taking his ace.

♡ 5 3

♡ Q 10 2 ■

Declarer leads low from dummy and plays the 9 from his hand. **Can declarer have J-9-x-x?** No, partner would win the trick with both the ace and king. **Can declarer have K-9-x-x?** No, he would put up his king, hoping for only one heart loser. **Can declarer have A-9-x-(x)?** Yes, he can and should.

♡ A 10 5

♡ K 7 6 2 ■

Declarer leads low from dummy and plays the queen from his hand, losing to your king. **Can declarer have Q-J-(x)?** No, then he would take a finesse against your king. Your partner holds the ♡ J.

$\heartsuit$ K 9 6 2 $\heartsuit$ A 7 4

Your opening lead of the $\heartsuit$ 2 is won by dummy's ace. **Can declarer have Q-x or Q-x-x?** Not unless he has fast discards available for his heart losers. Normally, he would duck the opening lead around to his queen. Your partner is likely to have the queen.

$\heartsuit$ K 9 7 5 2 $\heartsuit$ A Q 6

Your opening lead of the $\heartsuit$ 5 is won by dummy's ace. **Can declarer have x-x, x-x-x, or J-x?** Unlikely. Then he would probably finesse the queen or duck the lead to his jack. Unless declarer is about to take a fast discard for a losing heart, he probably has a singleton.

Let's look at situations at notrump.

$\heartsuit$ Q 6 2 $\heartsuit$ A J 9 5

Declarer leads low to dummy's 9, losing to partner's 10. **Can declarer have K-x-x-(x)?** No, he would play dummy's jack (or ace) in that event. Your partner has the $\heartsuit$ K.

$\heartsuit$ J 6 $\heartsuit$ K 9 5 2

Your partner's opening lead is the $\heartsuit$ 3. Declarer plays low from dummy and takes your king with the ace. **Can declarer have A-Q-x?** No, his proper play from dummy in that case would be the jack. **Can he have A-x-x?** No, he would play dummy's jack (and probably would duck your king, holding up his stopper). **Can he have A-10-x?** Yes.

$\heartsuit$ K 10 7 5 2 $\heartsuit$ A Q 6

You lead a heart, and declarer plays dummy's queen, winning the trick. **Can declarer have J-x-(x)?** No, then he would duck the lead to his hand. Your partner has the jack.

144

♡ A 6 4 2

■   ♡ K 7 3

Declarer leads low from dummy. **Can declarer have Q-J-10-x?** Surely not; then he could take a normal finesse. **Can he have J-10-9-x or Q-J-9-x?** Unlikely. Unless declarer is very short of entries, he would take finesses with these holdings. **Does your partner have an honor?** Yes. **Can declarer have Q-10-x-(x)?** Yes. **Can he have J-9-x-x or J-10-x-x?** Yes. Almost surely, you should play low.

♡ Q 4
♡ J 9 6 2   ■

Your opening lead is the ♡2 . . . queen, king, ace. **Can declarer have A-10-x-(x)?** No, he would play low from dummy to assure a second stopper. Your partner probably holds the ♡10 (although declarer could have the A-10 doubleton).

♡ Q 4

■   ♡ K 10 7 3

Partner's opening lead is a low heart, and declarer plays low from dummy. **Can declarer have A-x-x?** No, he would try dummy's queen at trick one, taking his only chance to take two tricks. **Can declarer have A-J-x?** No, his correct play from dummy would still be the queen, hoping to win and save his A-J tenace. Your partner is likely to have the ♡A. Put up your king, since declarer could hold J-x.

♡ K 9 3 2

■   ♡ A Q 4

Declarer leads low from dummy. **Can declarer have J-10-x?** No. Assuming that entries to his hand are no problem, he could take a finesse against the queen. **Can declarer have 10-6-5?** It's possible. **Can he have J-8-4?** Yes. In this case, you must duck smoothly. Declarer will probably finesse the 8, losing to partner's 10.

♡ A J 4 2

■   ♡ K 9 5 3

Declarer leads low from dummy. **Can declarer have Q-10-x?** No, with that he would finesse for the king. Partner should have an honor.

145

By ducking, you save a trick in the long run if declarer has Q-x or Q-x-x. Climb up with your king only if you desperately need a fast trick or quick entry.

Let's put one of these card combinations into a full deal.

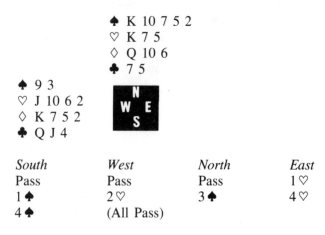

♠ K 10 7 5 2
♡ K 7 5
◊ Q 10 6
♣ 7 5

♠ 9 3
♡ J 10 6 2
◊ K 7 5 2
♣ Q J 4

South	West	North	East
Pass	Pass	Pass	1♡
1♠	2♡	3♠	4♡
4♠	(All Pass)		

You lead the ♡J, winning the first trick. Declarer ruffs the heart continuation. He leads a spade to the king, partner's queen falling, and continues with a club to his 10, losing to your jack. **What do you lead at this point?**

Partner would have won the club lead if he held the A-K, so declarer has one honor. It must be the ace, since declarer would put up the king, hoping for only one club loser. You know declarer has the ♠ AJ, so he cannot have the ◊ A. That would give him an opening bid. Leading a diamond from your king is safe at this point, and you may need to take your diamond tricks right away. The other hands are:

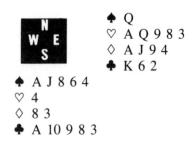

♠ Q
♡ A Q 9 8 3
◊ A J 9 4
♣ K 6 2

♠ A J 8 6 4
♡ 4
◊ 8 3
♣ A 10 9 8 3

Note that if the defenders do not cash out, declarer sets up his clubs with one ruff, discards two diamonds from dummy and loses only three tricks.

To review:

The ability to visualize how cards in a suit lie around the table and what will happen when the suit is led is called card sense. This ability can be acquired and developed. This chapter dealt with two areas of card combinations on defense.

First, the defenders often have card combinations that require correct handling. This may involve:

1. Unblocking a suit
2. Keeping communication
3. Preserving an entry
4. Making a surrounding play

Second, the defenders can infer declarer's holding in a suit (assuming declarer can be trusted to play logically) from his play. Drawing inferences — assumptions based on the logical analysis of evidence — is an essential part of reconstructing declarer's high cards, distribution and possible tricks.

QUIZ ON DEFENDERS' CARD COMBINATIONS

1.
    ♠ 10 5
    ♡ Q 7 5
    ◊ K Q 10 6 5
    ♣ A 9 2

               ♠ Q 9 7 2
       N   ♡ J 9 2
    W E   ◊ 8 7 4
       S   ♣ 10 8 6

South opened 1 NT, North raised to 3 NT. West leads the ♠4, and declarer wins your queen with the ace. Next declarer leads the ◊ J, won by partner's ace. Partner lays down the ♠J. What card do you play?

2.

♠ A Q 3
♡ A K 5 3
◇ 8 7
♣ J 9 7 4

♠ J 9 7
♡ 7 4 2
◇ A K J 10 6 4
♣ 8

North opened 1 ♣, you overcalled 2 ◇ (weak), South jumped to 3 NT. West leads the ◇ 9. How do you defend?

3.
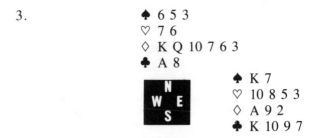
♠ 6 5 3
♡ 7 6
◇ K Q 10 7 6 3
♣ A 8

♠ K 7
♡ 10 8 5 3
◇ A 9 2
♣ K 10 9 7

South opened 1 NT, North raised to 3 NT. West leads the ♠Q. Plan your defense.

4.
♠ K 5
♡ Q J 7
◇ A Q 10 7 5
♣ J 7 4

♠ J 10 9 4
♡ K 5
◇ 9 8 3
♣ Q 10 8 3

South opened 1 ♡, North responded 2 ◇. South rebid 2 ♡, North raised to 4 ♡. You lead the ♠J. Dummy's king wins, and declarer passes the ♡Q to your king. What do you lead now?

5.

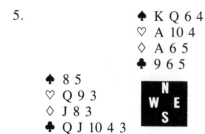

♠ K Q 6 4
♡ A 10 4
◇ A 6 5
♣ 9 6 5

♠ 8 5
♡ Q 9 3
◇ J 8 3
♣ Q J 10 4 3

South opened 1♠, North raised to 3♠, South jumped to 6♠. You lead the ♣Q. Declarer wins the king, draws two rounds of trumps (partner following), and leads the king, ace and another diamond, ruffing in his hand. Declarer then cashes the ♣A and puts you in with a third round of clubs, as partner discards a diamond. What do you lead?

6.

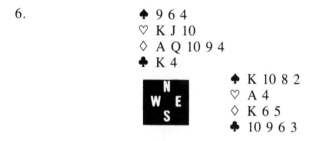

♠ 9 6 4
♡ K J 10
◇ A Q 10 9 4
♣ K 4

♠ K 10 8 2
♡ A 4
◇ K 6 5
♣ 10 9 6 3

South opened 1♣, North responded 1◇. South rebid 1 NT, North raised to 3 NT. West leads the ♡9. How do you defend?

SOLUTIONS TO QUIZ ON DEFENDERS' CARD COMBINATIONS

1. Partner's play of the ♠J suggests that he is preparing to cash his spade tricks. You must be careful to *unblock* the 7 or 9 on this trick. Partner's spade suit is K-J-6-4-3. Note what happens if you fail to unblock.
2. Play your ◇10 at trick one, letting declarer win but keeping communication with partner. If partner has a doubleton diamond and an entry, you can cash all your diamonds later. Keeping a link with partner is essential because you lack a side entry.
3. First, you must overtake the ♠Q to get out of partner's way. If you play low, declarer can win the first spade, blocking the suit. If you overtake, however, declarer must duck, else your side cashes spades when you win your ◇A. If declarer lets your

♠K win, shift to the ♣K, attacking dummy's entry to the diamonds. If you can keep declarer from using his diamonds, the contract will surely fail. (To return partner's suit is fruitless because he cannot have a fast entry to his spades. A count of high-card points tells you that partner has at most a queen outside spades.)

4. It is clear to shift to clubs, but you must be careful to lead the 10, a *surrounding* play. The club situation is:

```
              J 7 4
Q 10 8 3       ■           K 6 2
              A 9 5
```

Note what may happen if you lead low.

5. Assuming declarer has the ♡K and partner has the jack (the only time your play matters), you must lead the ♡Q. The heart position is:

```
              A 10 4
Q 9 3          ■           J 6 5 2
              K 8 7
```

Note the result if you lead the ♡3.

6. Win the ♡A and shift to the ♠10, a *surrounding* play. This is necessary if declarer holds ♠AJx and partner has ♠Qxx. Note what may happen if you lead low.

QUIZ ON INFERRING CARD COMBINATIONS

I. You are defending 4♡. Declarer has drawn trumps, leaving some in dummy. He then attacks the spade suit.

1.
```
              K J 9 4
A 7 3          ■
```

He leads low to dummy's 9, losing to partner's 10. Who has the ♠Q? How many spades does declarer have?

150

2.　　　　　　　7 5
　Q 10 6　　　■

He leads low from dummy to his 9, and you win the 10. Who has the ♠A? Who has the ♠K?

3.　　　　　　　7 6
　A J 5 2　　　■

He leads low from dummy and plays the 10 from hand, losing to your jack. Who has the ♠Q? Who has the ♠K?

4.　　　　　　　A 10 5
　K 7 6 2　　　■

He leads low from dummy to his queen, your king winning. Who has the ♠J?

In the remaining problems, the contract is *notrump*.

5.　　　　　　　A 10 5
　　　　　　　　■
　　　　　　　　　　K Q 6

Your partner leads the 4, and declarer goes right up with dummy's ace. Who has the jack?

6.　　　　　　　Q 5
　J 9 7 2　　　■

You lead the ♠2, and declarer puts up dummy's queen. Partner covers with the king, and declarer's ace wins. Who is likely to have the ♠10?

7.　　　　　　　Q 5
　　　　　　　　■
　　　　　　　　　　K 10 6 2

Partner leads the ♠4, and declarer plays low from dummy. Who has the ♠A?

SOLUTIONS TO QUIZ ON INFERRING CARD COMBINATIONS

1. Partner surely has the ♠Q. Declarer should have three or more spades. With only two spades, he would try for only one spade loser by playing the jack or king from dummy.
2. Declarer must have one of the high honors, since partner would *win the trick* with both the ace and king. If declarer had only the king, he would play it, hoping for one loser in the suit. So he should have the ace.
3. Declarer has one of the missing honors, since partner would *split* with the K-Q to assure one trick. But if declarer had only the king, he would play it, hoping for one loser in the suit. So declarer has the queen.
4. Partner has the ♠J, since declarer would take a finesse against your king if he held both the queen and jack.
5. Partner has the ♠J. If declarer held that card, he would duck the opening lead to his hand, hoping for two winners.
6. Partner is likely to have the ♠10, unless declarer's holding was specifically A-10 doubleton. If declarer's spades were A-10-x-(x), he could assure two tricks by playing low from dummy.
7. Partner is likely to have the ace. If declarer had ♠Axx or ♠AJx, he would put up the queen from dummy at trick one as his only chance to take a trick with that card. You should play the king because declarer's spade holding may be J-x.

Chapter 9

MORE ABOUT INFERENCES

A session of bridge is a series of little problems. You can solve some of them by applying rules and learned techniques, but others must be reasoned out from scratch. Bridge is a game of logic — an aptitude for problem-solving often means success.

An *inference* is an assumption based on evidence. You learned that a defender can often infer the lie of the cards from the way declarer plays a suit. Actually, if you can trust declarer to play logically, you can draw conclusions from the way he approaches the play of the *entire deal*. Other inferences are available from the *bidding* and partner's *opening lead*. Using every inference at your disposal helps you to reconstruct declarer's hand, an essential part of producing the best defense.

Let's see how the defenders can base their defense on the premise that declarer is playing the hand logically.

```
                    ♠ J 8 7 6 5
                    ♡ J 9 6 4
                    ◇ 7
                    ♣ A 7 6
    ♠ K Q 9             N
    ♡ 5            W        E
    ◇ K J 8 5 2         S
    ♣ 5 4 3 2
```

South	West	North	East
2 ♣ (1)	Pass	2 ◇ (2)	Pass
2 ♡	Pass	3 ♡	Pass
4 NT	Pass	5 ◇	Pass
7 ♡	(All Pass)		

(1) Strong, artificial
(2) Negative response

You lead your ♠K. Declarer wins the ace and reels off seven rounds of trumps (your partner had one trump). Next come the ♣A, ♣K and ♣Q. You can save two cards. **Do you keep the ◇K and ◇J or blank your ◇K to hang onto the ♠Q?**

153

Unless declarer has lost his mind, it is right to hold the ♠Q. It is pointless to save a diamond trick. If declarer had a diamond loser, *he would have ruffed it* in dummy before drawing trumps. Declarer's hand is:

♠ A 4
♡ A K Q 10 8 7 3
◊ A
♣ K Q 8

Drawing an inference from declarer's play may help you decide what *strategy* (see Chapter 4) to adopt.

1.

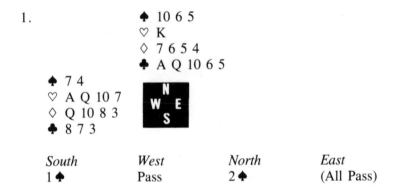

	♠ 10 6 5		
	♡ K		
	◊ 7 6 5 4		
	♣ A Q 10 6 5		
♠ 7 4			
♡ A Q 10 7			
◊ Q 10 8 3			
♣ 8 7 3			

South	West	North	East
1 ♠	Pass	2 ♠	(All Pass)

You lead the ◊ 3. East puts up the king, and declarer wins the ace. Declarer's next play is a heart, and you take your ace. **What do you lead now?**

A trump switch looks attractive — you can cut down on heart ruffs in dummy. But shouldn't you fear dummy's club suit? No, if declarer had the ♣K, he wouldn't be trying for heart ruffs in dummy. He would draw trumps and go after his club tricks. Declarer may well have a *singleton* club and plans to play a cross-ruff. Get a trump on the table. Declarer holds:

♠ K Q J 9 3
♡ 9 8 6 5
◊ A J 2
♣ 4

When partner wins the ace of trumps and returns a trump, declarer falls a trick short of his contract.

*KEEP YOUR EYES
AND EARS OPEN
AT ALL TIMES
FOR USEFUL
INFERENCES.*

2.

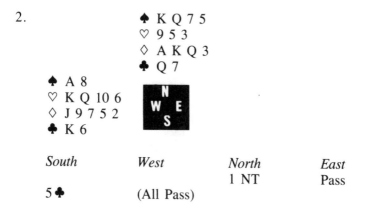

♠ K Q 7 5
♡ 9 5 3
◊ A K Q 3
♣ Q 7

♠ A 8
♡ K Q 10 6
◊ J 9 7 5 2
♣ K 6

South	West	North	East
		1 NT	Pass
5 ♣	(All Pass)		

You lead the ♡ K. Declarer wins the ace, leads a diamond to dummy and finesses the ♣ Q, losing to your king. **What do you lead?**

It looks routine to cash the ♡ Q, hoping the ♠ A will furnish the setting trick. But remember, it helps to put yourself in declarer's shoes and think how you would play in his place. Suppose declarer does have a losing heart. **How many diamonds must he have?** Suppose you as declarer had a heart loser and you had only one or two

155

diamonds. Wouldn't you cash dummy's high diamonds for a discard before you tried a finesse in trumps?

Declarer cannot have a heart loser unless he also had three diamonds. Return a diamond, hoping partner can ruff. Declarer's hand:

♠ 9 3
♡ A
◇ 10 8 4
♣ A J 10 9 5 4 2

3.

♠ J 8 6 4
♡ 7 5
◇ Q J 6
♣ K J 8 5

♠ K Q 10 5 2
♡ 10 4 2
◇ A 9 5
♣ A 4

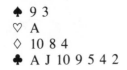

South	West	North	East
	1 ♠	Pass	Pass
Dbl	Pass	1 NT	Pass
4 ♡	(All Pass)		

You lead the ♠ K. Partner plays the 9, and declarer wins the ace. At trick two declarer leads a club toward dummy. **How do you defend?**

There is no point in ducking this trick to put declarer to a guess if he lacks the queen — he will play you for the ace because of your opening bid. But why has declarer led clubs at all? **Why hasn't he drawn trumps?** There is only one explanation — declarer wants to finesse in trumps and must get to dummy. You should win the ♣ A and cash the ♣ Q. Everyone follows. Now take your ◇ A and lead a third spade. Partner ruffs with his trump honor, promoting your ♡ 10. Declarer's hand:

♠ A 7
♡ A Q J 9 6 3
◇ K 10 4
♣ Q 3

156

Always look for an explanation when declarer delays drawing trumps.

4.

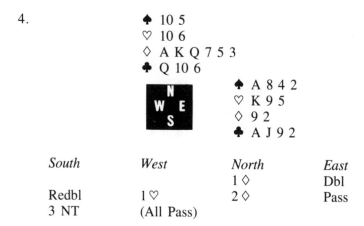

♠ 10 5
♥ 10 6
♦ A K Q 7 5 3
♣ Q 10 6

♠ A 8 4 2
♥ K 9 5
♦ 9 2
♣ A J 9 2

South	West	North	East
		1 ♦	Dbl
Redbl	1 ♥	2 ♦	Pass
3 NT	(All Pass)		

West leads the ♥3 . . . 10, king, ace. Declarer leads a diamond to the ace and the ♣10. **How do you defend?**

What does declarer have in hearts? A-x-x? Then he would hold up his stopper to break your communication. A-J-x? Then he would play low from dummy at trick one to assure a second stopper. Declarer must have the ace and queen. Since he also has six diamond tricks, he will be home if he takes a spade trick.

If declarer has the ♣K, he will play it if you duck the spade lead. Your only chance to beat the contract is to hop up with the ♣A and lead a low club. Declarer's hand:

♠ K Q J 3
♥ A Q 4
♦ 8 4
♣ 8 7 5 3

Valid inferences are also available from what happens (or doesn't happen) in the bidding.

5.

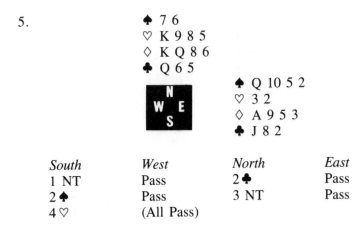

```
            ♠ 7 6
            ♡ K 9 8 5
            ◇ K Q 8 6
            ♣ Q 6 5
                            ♠ Q 10 5 2
                            ♡ 3 2
                            ◇ A 9 5 3
                            ♣ J 8 2
```

South	West	North	East
1 NT	Pass	2 ♣	Pass
2 ♠	Pass	3 NT	Pass
4 ♡	(All Pass)		

West leads the ◇ 10, and dummy's king is played. **How do you defend?**

Partner appears to have led from shortness. Can the ◇ 10 be a singleton? Not unless declarer opened a strange 1 NT! He promised four cards in each major, and if partner has led a singleton, declarer also has four diamonds, leaving him with a singleton club! So the lead is probably from 10-x. Since you have no other entry, you must duck the ◇ A. Perhaps partner has a fast reentry in trumps. Then he can lead his other diamond, and you can win and give him a ruff. Declarer's hand:

```
            ♠ A J 9 4
            ♡ Q J 7 4
            ◇ J 7 2
            ♣ A K
```

Counting and inference are tied together. When we discussed counting declarer's distribution, you learned that a count becomes available as play progresses and players fail to follow suit. Unfortunately, you may have a crucial decision *early* in the play. Still, you can try to *infer* the distribution from the bidding and the early play. We call this getting an *inferential count*.

6.

```
              ♠ Q 10 6 5
              ♡ Q 7 5
              ◊ A K 8 5
              ♣ K 8
♠ 3 2                        N
♡ A 10 8 6 2           W         E
◊ J 10 9                     S
♣ 7 5 3
```

South	West	North	East
		1 ◊	Pass
1 ♠	Pass	2 ♠	Pass
2 NT	Pass	4 ♠	(All Pass)

You lead the ◊ J. Declarer wins the queen in his hand and leads a spade to the queen and partner's king. Partner returns the ♡ 9, and declarer plays low. **How do you defend?**

Has partner led a singleton heart or from a doubleton? Let's try to work out declarer's hand. His 2 NT rebid was a game try, showing about 11 HCP but warning of poor spades. His hand is probably balanced (good for notrump). **Assuming declarer has only a four-card spade suit, can he also have four hearts?** No, then he would respond 1 ♡ to the opening bid, showing his suits *up the line*. So partner's ♡ 9 cannot be a singleton. You should duck your ace, playing partner for a doubleton heart and the ace of trumps. Declarer's hand:

```
♠ J 9 8 4
♡ K J 4
◊ Q 7 6
♣ A 10 4
```

Note that an inference rests on the assumption that an opponent is playing correctly. It is wrong to draw a subtle inference, basing it on declarer's skill, when he is a beginner. Try to play with and against strong players. That's the way to improve not only your skill at drawing inferences but your total game.

Remember the sources you can use to draw useful inferences:

1. DECLARER'S PLAY
2. THE BIDDING
3. PARTNER'S OPENING LEAD AND SUBSEQUENT PLAY

QUIZ ON DRAWING INFERENCES

1.
    ♠ Q 10 3
    ♡ A 7 4
    ◇ A Q 10 5 4
    ♣ 8 7

♠ K 4
♡ K 10 9 6 5 3
◇ 8 6
♣ A J 4

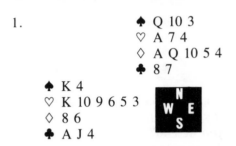

North opened 1◇, South responded 1♠. You overcalled 2♡. North raised to 2♠, and South jumped to 4♠. You lead the ♡10. Declarer wins dummy's ace and leads a spade to his ace and a spade back. You win the king, and partner's jack falls. What do you lead now?

2.
    ♠ 6 5
    ♡ A Q 6
    ◇ K 10 7 6 5
    ♣ K Q 5

♠ J 9 7 4 2
♡ K 5
◇ A 9 4 2
♣ A 10

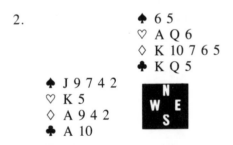

North opened 1◇, South responded 2♣. North raised to 3♣, South jumped to 5♣. You lead the ♠4. Declarer takes partner's king with the ace and leads a trump from his hand. How do you defend?

3.

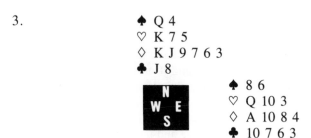

♠ Q 4
♥ K 7 5
♦ K J 9 7 6 3
♣ J 8

♠ 8 6
♥ Q 10 3
♦ A 10 8 4
♣ 10 7 6 3

South opened 1 NT, and North raised to 3 NT. West leads the ♥ 2. What is declarer's distribution?

4.

♠ 7 5
♥ A J 9 5
♦ K J 10 4
♣ Q 7 5

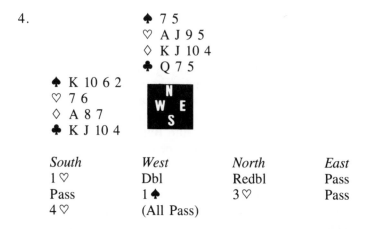

♠ K 10 6 2
♥ 7 6
♦ A 8 7
♣ K J 10 4

South	*West*	*North*	*East*
1 ♥	Dbl	Redbl	Pass
Pass	1 ♠	3 ♥	Pass
4 ♥	(All Pass)		

You lead a trump. Declarer wins and draws another round, your partner following low. Declarer then leads the ♦ Q, which you duck, and another diamond, which you win. What do you lead?

5.

♠ J 10 4
♥ K Q 7 6
♦ A K J 4
♣ 8 7

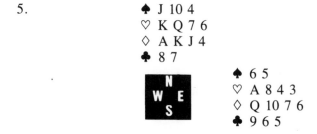

♠ 6 5
♥ A 8 4 3
♦ Q 10 7 6
♣ 9 6 5

South opened 1 ♠, North responded 2 ♦. South rebid 2 NT, North tried 3 ♠, South went on to 4 ♠. West leads the ♥ 9. How do you defend when declarer puts up dummy's ♥ K?

SOLUTIONS

1. Lead a low heart. Partner must have the $\heartsuit$ Q, since declarer would duck your lead to his hand if he started with Q-x. You hope partner can win and lead a club through declarer's holding.

2. Once partner shows the $\spadesuit$ K, declarer must have every other face card to justify his leap to an 11-trick contract. Your only chance is to take your trump ace and lead the $\diamondsuit$ A and another diamond, hoping partner can trump. Declarer's hand:

$\spadesuit$ A Q x
$\heartsuit$ x
$\diamondsuit$ Q J x
$\clubsuit$ J x x x x x

3. Declarer has *three hearts,* judging by partner's opening lead. Declarer has *five spades,* since partner would lead from a five-card spade suit in preference to a four-card heart suit after this auction. Declarer has *three clubs* at least, since partner would also lead from a five-card club suit. But declarer must have at least two diamonds for his 1 NT opening. Declarer's pattern, therefore, is 5-3-2-3. Simple, isn't it?

4. You can infer that declarer has four spades, since partner would have bid 1 $\spadesuit$ over North's redouble with four cards in that suit. (Even with a bad hand, partner would be duty-bound to confirm the best place to play.) You must lead a club. If declarer has losing clubs, they are about to go away on dummy's diamond winners. Notice that a club shift can't lose even if declarer has the ace! — he would discard his clubs on the diamonds anyway. If partner has the $\clubsuit$ A, however, you must lead a club now. Because declarer has four spades, you can wait to lead a spade even if your partner has the ace. Declarer can throw only two of his spades on the diamonds.

5. Duck the first trick. Partner's $\heartsuit$ 9 cannot be a singleton — declarer would have rebid 2 $\heartsuit$, not 2 NT, with a four-card heart suit. Perhaps partner has a doubleton heart and a high trump for a reentry.

Chapter 10

FALSE CARDS;
DECEPTION ON DEFENSE

In this chapter you will learn about an exciting part of defensive play: falsecarding and deception. To play a deft false card and cause declarer to fail in an easy contract is one of the biggest thrills in bridge.

Some players are so eager to be tricky that they overdo it. Here is the first thing to learn about deceptive defense.

Avoid frivolous false cards. Make deceptive plays only with a purpose.

Too often, you'll see a player indulge in something like this:

```
              ♠ 10 7 5 3
♠ Q J 4       ■              ♠ 9
              ♠ A K 8 6 2
```

Declarer, playing 4♠ with this trump suit, cashes the A-K of trumps. West falsecards (so to speak) with the queen on the second round. This accomplishes nothing, since declarer knows the situation; but East is apt to miscount declarer's distribution or the defenders' tricks.

The ideal false card fools declarer without fatally misleading partner.

A *false card* offers an opponent a losing option in the play or diverts him from making a winning play. One principle of falsecarding is that you can fool an opponent if you *play a card he already knows you hold (or will soon know you hold)*. Some of the following examples illustrate this principle.

1.
            K J 4
   Q 10 6   ■   8 5 3
            A 9 7 2

This is a well-known falsecarding position. Needing four tricks, declarer leads low to dummy's jack, winning. When declarer cashes the king next, *West must drop his queen.*

Suppose West plays the 10 instead. Declarer now leads the 4 toward his hand and, when East follows, goes up with the ace — he knows West still has the queen. After West plays the queen, however, declarer has a losing option — he can lead low to the 9, playing West for Q-6 and East for 10-8-5-3. *Note that our falsecarding principle applies;* West can gain by playing the queen, *the card he is known to hold,* under the king.

2.
            J 7 4 2
   10 9 5   ■   K 3
            A Q 8 6

This suit is trumps. Declarer leads low from dummy to his queen, winning. West *must* follow with the 9 or 10. Declarer now has a losing option — he can reenter dummy and lead the jack, hoping to pin West's doubleton 10-9. Note that without West's false card, declarer has no choice but to bang down the ace next.

3.
         ♠ 3
   ♠ J 10 5   ■   ♠ A 7
        ♠ K Q 9 8 6 4 2

Declarer winds up in 4 ♠ after opening 3 ♠ with his seven-card suit. He leads dummy's 3 and wins the king when East ducks. West must follow with the jack or 10. Declarer may then continue with the queen, trying to smother the doubleton J-10 in West. Note that if West doesn't falsecard, declarer will have no options — he must lead low on the second round, hoping to bring down the doubleton ace from East.

4.　　　　　　　A Q 7 5 2
　　　K J 4　　　　　10 9 3
　　　　　　　　8 6

Declarer needs to establish this suit at notrump. He finesses dummy's queen and cashes the ace. If West follows with the king (the card he is known to hold) on the second round, he may persuade declarer that the suit is splitting unfavorably.

These situations illustrate mandatory or *obligatory* false cards. A defender *must* falsecard, else declarer is bound to make the winning play. In the next example, a defender falsecards merely to plant a seed of doubt in declarer's mind.

5.　　　　　　　A J 7 6 4
　　　Q 9 2　　　■　　　10 8
　　　　　　　　K 5 3

Needing tricks from this suit, declarer cashes the king. East fears that declarer is about to finesse against West's queen, so he drops the *10*. Declarer may try to drop the doubleton queen instead of finessing.

6.
<pre>
            A K J 9 7 5
  8 6 2   ■   Q 10
            4 3
</pre>

Declarer cashes dummy's ace, and East drops the *queen.* Declarer will probably come back to his hand and lead low to the 9, playing West for 10-8-6-2. Of course, declarer may go wrong even if East plays the 10. Declarer may suspect East of playing the 10 from 10-x to dissuade a finesse against the queen. But the play of the queen by East is almost sure to work.

A similar position, but with an obligatory false card, is:

<pre>
            A J 8 7 5
  Q 10   ■   6 3 2
            K 9 4
</pre>

Declarer leads the 4 toward dummy. West puts up his *queen.* Declarer wins dummy's ace and leads low to the 9 next, playing East for 10-6-3-2.

<pre>
            ♠ J 9 4
  ♠ 8 6 3   ■   ♠ Q 10
            ♠ A K 7 5 2
</pre>

Playing 4♠ with this trump suit, declarer leads low from dummy. East plays the *queen,* the card he will soon be known to hold. Declarer wins and leads low to dummy's 9 next.

Several false cards are associated with the *doubleton J-9.* Look for a chance to falsecard with this combination.

7.
<pre>
            10 8 4
  K 5 2   ■   J 9
            A Q 7 6 3
</pre>

Declarer leads the 4 from dummy. If East follows with the 9, declarer finesses the queen, losing to the king, but leads the ace next to drops East's jack. Note the effect if East plays the jack on the first round. Declarer will still lose a finesse with the queen, but he will lead low to dummy's 8 next, playing West for K-9-5-2.

False cards are also available with A-J-9 and K-J-9.

```
              Q 8 3
  7 5 4        ■          A J 9
              K 10 6 2
```

Declarer leads low from dummy, intending to finesse his 10. East plays the *jack*. When declarer's king wins, he will lead low to dummy's 8 next. (Note that East's play can't cost, no matter who has the missing 10.)

You even have a chance to falsecard with Q-J-9.

```
8.            K 10 8
  A 5 4 3      ■          Q J 9
              7 6 2
```

Declarer needs one trick from this suit. He leads low toward dummy and makes the percentage play of the 8 when West ducks. If East wins his 9, declarer has no option but to lead to dummy's king next. But East wins the *jack,* and declarer can then continue his plan by leading low to the 10 next.

```
9.            ♠ A Q 5
  ♠ 4          ■          ♠ K 10 8 6
              ♠ J 9 7 3 2
```

Playing 4 ♠ with this trump suit, declarer leads low to dummy's queen. Suppose East wins the king. Declarer will cash the ace next, of course, and follow with the marked finesse against East's 10, bringing in the suit.

To have a chance for two tricks, East must refuse the first trick, falsecarding with the *8.* If declarer is convinced that East has the doubleton 10-8, he will come back to his hand and lead the jack, hoping to pin the 10. Suddenly, East's holding will be worth two tricks.

```
10.           ♠ Q 10 8 5
  ♠ J 9 6 2    ■          ♠ 4
              ♠ A K 7 3
```

Declarer plays 4 ♠ , having arrived in a 4-4 fit by way of Stayman. He cashes the king of trumps. West *must* follow with the *9.* If West plays low, declarer will continue with the ace, guarding against J-9-x-x with West. (Declarer is helpless if *East* has J-9-x-x.) If West falsecards, however, declarer may lead to the queen next, playing West for the *singleton* 9 and East for J-x-x-x.

11.

	Q 9 7 6 4	
K J 10	■	8 5 2
	A 3	

At notrump declarer considers setting up this suit. He cashes the ace, intending to lead to the queen next, hoping for a 3-3 split with the king onside. West, who sees what is coming, drops his *king* under the ace! Declarer will look elsewhere for tricks.

For a change, let's look at a full deal.

12.

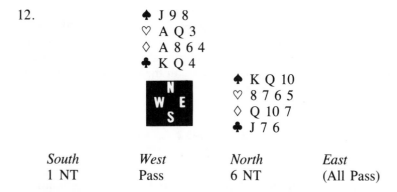

♠ J 9 8
♡ A Q 3
◇ A 8 6 4
♣ K Q 4

♠ K Q 10
♡ 8 7 6 5
◇ Q 10 7
♣ J 7 6

South	West	North	East
1 NT	Pass	6 NT	(All Pass)

West leads a low spade against the slam, and declarer plays the 8 from dummy. **How do you defend?**

Declarer is marked with all the missing high cards. He is likely to have 12 tricks, especially since the diamond finesse will work for him. You must offer him an alternative to finessing in diamonds. Play your ♠K (or ♠Q) at trick one. The missing hands:

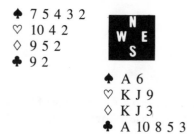

♠ 7 5 4 3 2
♡ 10 4 2
◇ 9 5 2
♣ 9 2

♠ A 6
♡ K J 9
◇ K J 3
♣ A 10 8 5 3

He will win the ♠ A, test clubs and, needing just one more trick, lead a spade to dummy's 9. Notice what happens if East plays the ♠ 10 at trick one. Declarer is forced to try the diamond finesse, which works so well that he takes 13 tricks.

Now we will look at other situations that give the defenders a chance for deceptive play. Not every case involves a true false card.

1.
$\quad\quad\quad\quad\quad$ ♡ 7 6
$\quad$ ♡ J 9 4 2 $\quad$ ■ $\quad\quad$ ♡ A K 8 3
$\quad\quad\quad\quad\quad$ ♡ Q 10 5

West leads the ♡ 2 against notrump. East wins the *ace* and returns the 3, giving declarer a tough guess. Notice that East's play *cannot cost*. East knows that declarer has three (or more) hearts from West's lead of the 2.

2.
$\quad\quad\quad\quad\quad$ ♡ K Q 10
$\quad$ ♡ J 9 4 2 $\quad$ ■ $\quad\quad$ ♡ A 8 3
$\quad\quad\quad\quad\quad$ ♡ 7 6 5

West leads the ♡ 2 against notrump. Declarer puts up dummy's king, and East should duck without hesitation. When West leads a heart again (or if declarer must try for a second heart trick), declarer must guess whether to play the queen or 10. Declarer can't go wrong if East takes the ace at the first trick.

Although the defenders are handicapped by not seeing each other's hands, they have a compensating advantage: they know whether declarer's finesses will work, whether his key suits will split and whether his whole plan of play will succeed. How do you defend this deal?

3.

　　　　　　　♠ A Q 10 7 6
　　　　　　　♡ A J 6
　　　　　　　◊ A K J
　　　　　　　♣ 7 6

♠ J 5 2
♡ 10 9 8 7
◊ Q 7 6
♣ A J 10

South	West	North	East
	Pass	1 ♠	Pass
2 NT	Pass	6 NT	(All Pass)

You lead the ♡ 10. Declarer wins dummy's jack and leads a club to his king. **What do you do?**

The bidding marks declarer with all the missing high cards, so he has five spade tricks, at least three hearts (you must assume he has only three; otherwise, there is no defense), two diamonds and one club. Suppose you win the club. Declarer will then know he has only one club trick, so he will take the diamond finesse. It will work, and he will score the slam.

Now say you *duck* the ♣K. Declarer won't know what to do. If the ♣A is onside, he can take the 12th trick by leading a club to the queen. He has no reason to shift to diamonds.

Notice that *table presence* is a factor. Unless you play a low club *in tempo*, declarer will know you have the ace. Your best chance to play smoothly when the crucial moment comes is to do your thinking and planning in advance.

Declarer's hand is:

　　　　　　　♠ K 8 3
　　　　　　　♡ K Q 4
　　　　　　　◊ 10 8 5 3
　　　　　　　♣ K Q 2

A common deceptive technique arises when declarer has a repeatable finesse that loses. In such a case, a defender may let declarer's first finesse work, reserving a nasty surprise for later. This example is given by Alfred Sheinwold:

4.

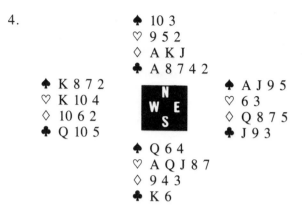

```
            ♠ 10 3
            ♡ 9 5 2
            ◊ A K J
            ♣ A 8 7 4 2
♠ K 8 7 2                    ♠ A J 9 5
♡ K 10 4        N           ♡ 6 3
◊ 10 6 2     W     E        ◊ Q 8 7 5
♣ Q 10 5        S           ♣ J 9 3
            ♠ Q 6 4
            ♡ A Q J 8 7
            ◊ 9 4 3
            ♣ K 6
```

South was declarer at 4♡. West led the ♠2, and the defenders played three rounds of the suit, forcing dummy to ruff. Declarer led a trump to his jack, and West ducked without a hitch. Declarer then went back to dummy with a high diamond and led a second trump to his queen. This time West won and returned a diamond, and declarer had to lose a diamond for down one.

What happens if West wins the *first* round of trumps? Declarer wins the diamond shift, draws trumps and leads three rounds of clubs, ruffing the third. This sets up dummy's clubs, and a high diamond remains in dummy as an entry. By ducking the first trump lead, West induced declarer to use one of his precious entries for the wrong reason.

Another common deceptive technique is *winning a trick with a higher card than necessary.*

5.

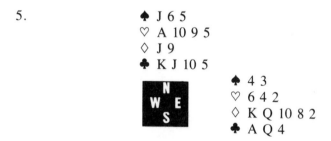

```
            ♠ J 6 5
            ♡ A 10 9 5
            ◊ J 9
            ♣ K J 10 5
                            ♠ 4 3
                N           ♡ 6 4 2
            W       E       ◊ K Q 10 8 2
                S           ♣ A Q 4
```

South opened 1 NT and plays 3 NT. West leads the ♠9. Declarer wins the 10 and leads the ♣9, ducking in dummy. **How do you defend?**

Win the ♣A(!) and shift to the ◇K. What happens if you win the ♣Q and shift to the ◇K? Declarer will be forced to play hearts to make his contract, and you can see that a heart finesse will work. Make declarer think his *club* finesse has worked! The missing hands:

♠ 9 8 7 2
♡ K 8 7
◇ 7 5 3
♣ 8 6 2

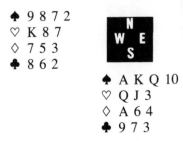

♠ A K Q 10
♡ Q J 3
◇ A 6 4
♣ 9 7 3

How do you defend this deal?

6.

♠ K J 10 5
♡ K 5
◇ K 8 5
♣ 10 9 7 3

♠ Q 6
♡ Q J 10 9
◇ 9 6 3
♣ A Q 4 2

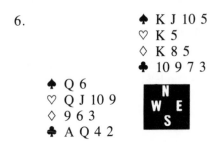

South plays 3 NT after opening 1 NT. You lead the ♡Q. Dummy's king wins, and declarer immediately leads the ♣10, playing low from his hand. You take the ♣Q and continue with the ♡10. Declarer ducks and wins your ♡J continuation with the ace. Now declarer leads the ♣K. **What do you do?**

Declarer has at least eight tricks (two in each suit), since he must hold the ♣A and ◇A on the bidding. Assuming partner has a diamond stopper, declarer must guess the ♠Q for his contract. You can compel him to misguess if you win the ♣A and *return a club*, as though your hearts were Q-J-10.

Declarer will now take the spade finesse through your partner because he thinks you don't have a winner to cash. Then you can take the ♡9 for the setting trick.

We stressed that a good false card fools an opponent without fatally misleading partner. Rarely, it is best to feed partner false information. A good defender is aware of his partner's problems and tries to help him. If the way to do this is to *deceive* him, so be it.

7.

♠ Q 6
♡ K J 4
◇ A K 10 6 4
♣ 8 7 6

	N	
W		E
	S	

♠ 8 3
♡ A Q
◇ 9 5 2
♣ K Q J 5 4 3

South	West	North	East
		1 ◇	2 ♣
2 ♠	Pass	3 ◇	Pass
3 ♠	Pass	4 ♠	(All Pass)

West leads the ♣9. **Which club do you play in third seat?**
Since you want a heart shift if partner gains the lead, you must make him think there is no future in clubs. Play the ♣K, denying the queen. If partner wins a trick, he will have no choice but to shift to hearts. Perhaps you can cash two hearts and a club. Declarer's hand could be:

♠ A J 10 9 7 4
♡ 10 5
◇ Q J 3
♣ A 10

To review:

A false card offers an opponent a losing option in the play or diverts him from the winning play. Some false cards are *obligatory;* unless a defender falsecards, declarer can't go wrong.

Avoid frivolous false cards. Make deceptive plays only with a definite purpose. A good false card fools an opponent without fatally misleading partner. If you get too enthusiastic and falsecard aimlessly, you will have many debacles and few victories. Save your false cards for positions you have studied.

Aside from the standard falsecarding positions, the defenders have many other chances to lead declarer astray. Some deceptive techniques are:

1. Letting declarer win the first time he tries a repeatable finesse.
2. Winning a trick with a higher card than necessary.
3. Declining to cash a winner at the first opportunity.
4. Underleading winners or intermediates to make declarer guess.
5. Ducking deceptively.

Again, remember that a deceptive play must have a purpose. Do not play deceptive cards at random.

QUIZ ON FALSE CARDS AND DECEPTION

1.

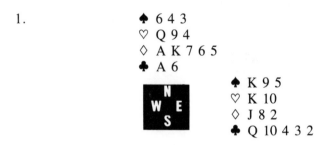

♠ 6 4 3
♡ Q 9 4
◇ A K 7 6 5
♣ A 6

♠ K 9 5
♡ K 10
◇ J 8 2
♣ Q 10 4 3 2

South opened 1 ♡ , North responded 2 ◇ . South rebid 2 NT, North jumped to 4 ♡. West leads the ♠ 2. Declarer wins your ♠ K with the ace, leads a club to dummy's ace and a heart from dummy. What do you play?

2.

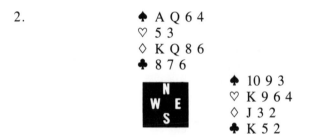

♠ A Q 6 4
♡ 5 3
◇ K Q 8 6
♣ 8 7 6

♠ 10 9 3
♡ K 9 6 4
◇ J 3 2
♣ K 5 2

South opened 1 NT, North responded 2 ♣ . South rebid 2 ♠ , North raised to 4 ♠ . West leads the ♣ J, won by declarer's queen. At trick two declarer leads a low spade to dummy's queen. What do you play?

3.

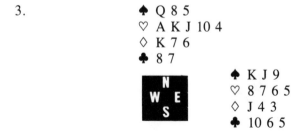

♠ Q 8 5
♡ A K J 10 4
◇ K 7 6
♣ 8 7

♠ K J 9
♡ 8 7 6 5
◇ J 4 3
♣ 10 6 5

South opened 1 ♠ , North responded 2 ♡ . South rebid 2 NT, North jumped to 4 ♠ . West cashes the ♣ A and ♣K and shifts to the ◇ 10, won by dummy's king. Declarer then leads a low trump from dummy. What do you play?

4.
♠ A Q 7 6 3
♥ K 7 6
♦ A J 7
♣ 10 4

♠ K J 9
♥ Q 10 5 3
♦ 9 8
♣ K Q 9 5

North opened 1 ♣ , South responded 2 ♣ . North rebid 2 ♠ , South tried 2 NT, North raised to 3 NT. You lead the ♥ 3. Partner plays the jack, and declarer wins the ace. Declarer then leads a spade to dummy's queen and continues with the ♠ A. What do you play?

5.
♠ Q 8 6 5 2
♥ K 7 6
♦ A 8 7
♣ A 5

♠ K J 9
♥ Q 10 8 3 2
♦ J 6
♣ K J 4

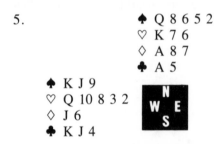

North opened 1 ♠ , South responded 1 NT and all passed. You lead the ♥ 3. Partner plays the jack, and declarer wins the ace. Next, declarer lays down the ♠ A — not the card you wanted to see. What do you play?

6.
♠ 5
♥ A K Q 5
♦ K 7 5 3
♣ A 8 6 4

♠ A 7 4
♥ J 7 4
♦ Q J 10
♣ J 9 5 3

South opened 3 ♠ , North raised to 4 ♠ . You lead the ♦ Q, winning the first trick. Your ♦ J holds the second trick, but declarer ruffs the third diamond. He then leads a heart to dummy and a spade toward his hand. Partner plays the 10, declarer the king. How do you defend?

7.
♠ 7 4
♡ A Q 4
◇ K Q 10 6 5
♣ 8 7 6

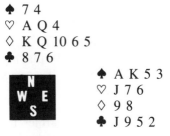

♠ A K 5 3
♡ J 7 6
◇ 9 8
♣ J 9 5 2

South opened 1 NT, North raised to 3 NT. West leads the ♠2. How do you defend?

8.
♠ 6 5
♡ J 4 3 2
◇ 8 7 6 5 4
♣ A K

♠ A Q
♡ 10 8 6 5
◇ J 3
♣ Q J 10 8 5

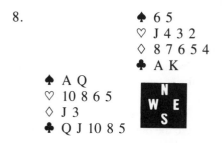

South opened 1 ♠, North responded 1 NT; South rebid 3 ♠, North raised to 4 ♠. You lead the ♣Q. Dummy wins, and declarer continues with a trump to his jack. How do you defend?

SOLUTIONS

1. Play the *king*. Declarer is likely to have A-J-x-x-x. He will win his ace and lead to dummy's 9, playing you for the singleton king and partner for 10-x-x-x. If, as expected, declarer has the missing heart honors, a false card is your only chance to win a trick.

2. Play the *9* (or 10). If your partner has the king of trumps, declarer will be tempted to come back to his hand and lead the jack, hoping to pin the doubleton 10-9 in your hand.

3. Play the *jack*. This will cost nothing if partner has the 10. If declarer's spades are A-10-x-x-x, he will win and lead low to dummy's 8 on the second round, playing you for the singleton jack or the doubleton K-J.

4. Drop the *king,* the card you are known to hold. You hope to persuade declarer that the spades are not splitting evenly. Perhaps he will switch to clubs.

5. Drop your ♠K under the ace. Declarer may think the spades are breaking badly and look for tricks elsewhere.

6. Duck smoothly. Partner may have the doubleton J-10 of trumps. If you duck, declarer must guess how to continue. He may lead a *low* spade next, hoping to bring down the ace. Note that if you win the first spade, declarer has no option but to bang down the queen later.

7. Win the ♠A and return the ♠3, putting declarer to a tough guess if his spades are Q-10-x. This play cannot cost, since declarer is known to have at least three spades from partner's lead of the *2*.

8. Win the ♠A(!) and return a club. You hope to persuade declarer to use his last entry to dummy for another *spade* finesse. If you win the ♠Q, declarer will use the remaining entry to take a possible finesse in a red suit. Declarer's hand is:

> ♠ K J 10 x x x x
> ♡ K Q
> ◇ A Q
> ♣ x x

COMPREHENSIVE GLOSSARY

"ABOVE THE LINE": Scoring of points won for overtricks, penalties and bonuses.

ACTIVE DEFENSE: The defenders' approach when they are desperate for tricks because declarer threatens to get discards for his losers.

ASSUMPTION: Technique by which declarer or defender bases his play on the premise that the contract can be made or set.

ATTITUDE: Defensive signal that shows like or dislike for a suit.

AVOIDANCE: Technique in play whereby a dangerous opponent is kept from gaining the lead.

AUCTION: See BIDDING.

BALANCED HAND: Hand containing no void suit or singleton, and no more than one doubleton.

BALANCING: Backing into the auction after the opponents have stopped low, counting on partner to hold some values.

"BELOW THE LINE":	Scoring of points that count toward making a game.
BID:	Call in the auction that promises to take a certain number of tricks in the play and suggests a suit as trumps (or suggests the play be at notrump).
BIDDING:	The first phase of each hand of bridge, when the players on both sides have a chance to bid for the right to name the trump suit and suggest how many tricks they expect their side to win in the play.
BLACKWOOD:	A conventional bid of 4 NT that asks partner to reveal, through an artificial response, the number of aces he holds.
BOOK:	(1) The first six tricks won by declarer's side; (2) the number of tricks the defenders must win before they begin to score undertricks.
BROKEN SEQUENCE:	Sequence such as QJ9, which contains a gap between the middle and lowest of the three cards.
BROKEN SUIT:	Suit which contains no cards adjacent in rank.
BUSINESS DOUBLE:	Penalty double.
CALL:	Any action, including a pass, taken in the bidding.
CAPTAINCY:	The bidding principle whereby one partner is obliged to take responsibility for placing the contract once his partner's hand is limited in strength.
CARD SENSE:	An intangible quality that those skilled in card play seem to possess.
CHICAGO SCORING:	A type of scoring in which every deal is taken as a separate entity. There are no rubbers or partscores carried over the next deal.
COME-ON:	An encouraging attitude signal.
COMPETITIVE BIDDING:	Auctions in which both sides bid.
CONSTRUCTIVE BIDDING:	Auctions in which one side tries to reach its best contract without interference.
CONTRACT:	The number of tricks that the side that wins the auction undertakes to make.
CONTROL:	Holding that prevents the opponents from taking two fast tricks in that suit. An ace; king; or singleton or void, if some other suit is trumps.
CONVENTION:	A bid to which an artificial meaning has been assigned.
CROSS-RUFF:	A play technique in which cards are trumped in both partnership hands alternately, on several successive tricks.

CUEBID:	(1) A bid of an opponent's suit, intended to show great strength. (2) A bid of a suit in which a control is held, intended to facilitate slam investigation. (3) Any of several conventional cuebids, such as Michaels.
CUT:	The division of the pack into rough halves prior to the deal.
DEAL:	The distribution of the 52 cards, 13 to each player face down, that begins each hand of bridge.
DECLARER:	The player who tries to make the contract by using both his own and dummy's cards.
DEFENDERS:	The partnership that opposes declarer and tries to defeat the contract.
DISCARD:	A played card which is not of the suit led nor of the trump suit.
DOUBLE:	A call generally intended to increase the penalty suffered by the opponents if their last bid becomes an unsuccessful çontract.
DOUBLE FINESSE:	A combination of plays in which declarer finesses against two missing honors.
DOUBLE SQUEEZE:	An advanced type of squeeze in which each defender is squeezed in turn.
DOUBLETON:	A holding of two cards in a suit.
DRAW TRUMPS:	Technique in which declarer leads trumps, forcing the opponents to follow suit, until their trumps are exhausted.
DROP:	Cause a missing high card to fall by playing a still higher card or cards.
DUMMY:	Declarer's partner. The term is also applied to the dummy's cards, placed face up on the table.
DUMMY REVERSAL:	Technique by which declarer makes extra tricks by ruffing several times in his own hand and ultimately drawing trumps with dummy's trump holding.
DUPLICATE BRIDGE:	A contest in which the same hands are played several times by different players, allowing for a comparison of results.
DUPLICATION OF VALUES:	The condition in which the high cards and distribution of the partnership hands are ill-suited to each other.
ECHO:	A high-low sequence of play used to signal attitude or count.
ENDPLAY:	Technique by which a trick is gained through deliberately giving an opponent the lead in a position where he has no safe exit.
ENTRY:	A card used as a means of gaining the lead.
EQUALS:	Cards that are adjacent in rank, or that become adjacent when the cards that separate them are played.

FALSE CARD:	A card played with intent to deceive.
FALSE PREFERENCE:	A preference offered without true support, typically with two cards.
FINESSE:	Maneuver by which it is hoped to win a trick with an intermediate card, by playing that card after one opponent has already played.
FIT:	A holding which suggests that suit will adequately serve as trumps.
FIVE-CARD MAJORS:	A bidding style in which an opening bid of 1 ♠ or 1 ♡ promises five or more cards.
FOLLOWING SUIT:	Each player's first obligation in the play, to play a card of the same suit that was led to the trick if possible.
FORCING BID:	A bid that compels partner to take further action.
FORCING DEFENSE:	The defenders' approach when they try to exhaust declarer of trumps by repeatedly forcing him to ruff.
FORCING PASS:	Pass made over an opponent's bid, which compels partner to double the opponents or bid further.
FREE BID:	Bid made when the alternative would be to pass and allow partner the next opportunity to act. Typically based on sound values.
FREE RAISE:	Raise of partner's suit in competition. Not a significant term, since such a raise does *not* imply extra strength.
GAME:	(1) A unit of scoring, two of which comprise a rubber; a game is won by the first partnership to score 100 or more points below the line.
	(2) Any contract which will allow the partnership to score game if fulfilled.
GAME TRY:	A bid that suggests interest in game and asks partner to assess his values and make the final decision.
GERBER:	A conventional bid of 4 ♣ that asks partner to reveal, through an artificial response, the number of aces he holds.
GRAND SLAM FORCE:	A bid of 5 NT, when used to show interest in bidding a grand slam in the agreed trump suit provided partner holds certain honors in trumps.
HIGH-CARD POINT COUNT:	Method of hand evaluation in which a numerical value is assigned to each high honor.
HONOR:	Ace, king, queen, jack or ten.
HONORS:	Bonus available in the scoring for a holding of four or all five honors in the trump suit in the same hand; or, at notrump, all four aces in the same hand.
HOLD-UP:	Refusal to take a winner, often for purposes of disrupting the opponents' communication.
INFERENCE:	A conclusion logically deduced from evidence.

INFERENTIAL COUNT:	An assessment of the entire distribution of the concealed hands, based on evidence from the bidding and the early play.
INTERIOR SEQUENCE:	Holding such as KJ109x, in which the equals are accompanied by some higher card.
INTERMEDIATES:	Cards which may become winners as the cards that outrank them are played.
INVITATIONAL BID:	Bid that asks partner to continue to game or slam with maximum values.
JORDAN:	The conventional understanding in which a jump to 2 NT by responder, after the opener's bid is doubled for takeout, shows a limit raise in opener's suit.
JUMP OVERCALL:	A suit bid made usually (as the next bid) after an opponent has opened the bidding, but at a higher level than necessary.
JUMP SHIFT:	(1) A jump of one level in a new suit by opening bidder. (2) A jump of one level in a new suit by responder. Either action implies great strength.
LEG:	A fulfilled partscore, a step toward game.
LEAD:	The first card played to a trick.
LIMIT BID:	Bid that promises no more than a pre-agreed amount of high-card strength.
LIMIT RAISE:	Direct double raise of partner's opening one-bid that promises invitational values only.
LONG CARDS:	Low cards that become winners because they are the only cards of their suit which remain in play.
MAJOR SUITS:	Spades and hearts.
MATCHPOINT SCORING:	Type of scoring used in duplicate (tournament) bridge, in which several different results from an identical deal are compared.
MAXIMUM:	Holding the greatest possible values for one's previous bidding.
MINIMUM:	Holding the fewest possible values for one's previous bidding.
NEGATIVE RESPONSE:	Bid, often artificial, that denies good values; made in response to partner's forcing action.
NOTRUMP:	Strain in which the play is conducted with no trump suit. The highest card played of the suit that is led to a trick wins that trick.
OBLIGATORY FALSECARD:	Falsecard that will lead to a certain loss if not played.
OBLIGATORY FINESSE:	The handling of certain suit combinations in which declarer plays a low card from both hands, hoping his opponent will be forced to follow suit with a high honor.
OFFSIDE:	Unfavorably placed for a finesse to work.

ONSIDE:	Favorably placed for a finesse to work.
OPEN THE BIDDING:	To make the first bid in the auction.
OPENING LEAD:	The lead to the first trick, made by the defender to declarer's left.
OVERCALL:	Bid in a suit after the opponents have opened the bidding (but before partner has taken any action).
OVERTRICKS:	Tricks taken in excess of those bid.
PARTIAL:	A partscore.
PARTNERSHIP:	Two players working as a unit. Bridge is played by two competing partnerships. Partners sit opposite each other. Trust and cooperation between partners are important features of the game.
PARTSCORE:	A contract below the level of game. Successful partscores can accumulate toward scoring game.
PASS:	Call in the auction when the player does not wish to bid, double or redouble.
PASSED OUT:	Deal on which none of the four players bid. Calls for another deal.
PASSIVE DEFENSE:	Defenders' approach when dummy is short of winners and the defense can wait on its tricks.
PENALTY DOUBLE:	Double made for a larger penalty, in the expectation that the contract will fail.
PERCENTAGE PLAY:	Line of play which will succeed most often, determined on only a mathematical basis.
PLAIN SUIT:	Any suit other than trumps.
POINT COUNT:	The method of hand evaluation whereby a numerical value is assigned to the possible trick-taking features of a hand.
POSITIVE RESPONSE:	Response to partner's forcing opening that promises certain good values.
PREEMPTIVE BID:	Bid made not for constructive purposes but merely to crowd the opponents and make it hard for them to bid accurately.
PREFERENCE:	A bid which chooses between two possible strains partner has offered.
PREPARED BID:	An opening bid in a low-ranking suit (often, a suit of only three cards), made so that a higher-ranking suit will provide an easy, space-saving rebid.
PRIMARY VALUES:	Aces and kings.
PROPRIETIES:	That section of the Laws of Contract Bridge that deals with ethics and etiquette.

PSYCHIC BID:	A bluff bid, made on a non-existent suit or without values, intended to intimidate the opposition.
QUANTITATIVE SLAM (GAME) TRY:	Bid that asks partner to pass or bid on, based strictly on the number of high-card values he holds.
RAISE:	A bid in the same suit (or notrump) that partner has just bid, often confirming that suit as trumps.
REBID:	(1) Bid the same suit a second time. (2) Any bid chosen at one's second turn.
REDOUBLE:	Call available in the auction which doubles, in turn, points scored if the contract is played doubled.
RESPONDER:	Opening bidder's partner.
RESTRICTED CHOICE:	A mathematical concept, based on the opponents' possible play from a holding of several equal cards, that may be helpful in determining the play of certain suit combinations.
REVERSE:	(1) A rebid in a new suit, such that the level of the contract will be increased if partner shows a preference for the first suit. (2) To bid in such a way, thereby showing a strong hand.
REVOKE:	Failure to follow suit when holding a card of the suit led.
RUBBER:	Unit of scoring in bridge, won by the side to first make two games, and carrying a large bonus.
RUFF:	To trump.
RUFF-AND-DISCARD (RUFF-SLUFF):	The lead of a suit in which both declarer and dummy are void, allowing declarer to discard a loser from the hand of his choice while he ruffs in the other.
RULE OF 11:	Device, applicable if the lead is known to be fourth-highest, that may be used to make judgments in the play. Subtract the rank of the spot led from 11. The remainder shows the number of higher cards held by the hands, other than leader's.
SACRIFICE:	A deliberate overbid, but one in which declarer expects to be penalized fewer points than the opponents would score if allowed to play their own contract.
SAFETY PLAY:	The handling of a combination of cards so as to insure against a devastating loss of tricks.
SECOND-HAND:	(1) The next player to have a chance to bid after the dealer. (2) The player who plays immediately after a trick is led to.
SECONDARY VALUES:	Queens and jacks.
SEMI-BALANCED HAND:	Hand which is neither balanced nor unbalanced by definition, 2-2-4-5 or 2-2-3-6 pattern.
SEQUENCE:	Three or more cards adjacent in rank, the highest one of which is an honor.

SET:	To defeat the contract.
SHORT CLUB:	See PREPARED BID.
SHUT-OUT BID:	A preemptive bid.
SIGNAL:	Any of several conventional understandings through which the defenders can give each other information by means of the card they play.
SIGNOFF:	Bid that suggests that partner pass.
SIMPLE SQUEEZE:	Type of squeeze in which a single opponent is squeezed.
SINGLETON:	A holding of only one card in a suit.
SLAM:	A contract for 12 or 13 tricks, carrying a bonus in the scoring.
SPOT CARD:	Card below the rank of an honor.
SQUEEZE:	Technique, most often used by declarer, in which a defender is forced to relinquish a winner no matter what card he chooses.
STANDARD AMERICAN:	The bidding system most commonly used in America; essentially, the Goren style, with gadgets and refinements added.
STOPPER:	A card or combination of cards certain to produce a trick in a suit.
STRIP:	Play a suit or suits so as to make it impossible for an opponent to lead that suit or lead it safely.
SUIT-PREFERENCE SIGNAL:	Defensive signal which bears no relation to its own suit but shows interest in another, specific suit.
SURROUNDING PLAY:	Maneuver in which a defender breaks a suit by leading a high card that is part of a near-sequential holding.
SYSTEM:	The total framework in which the partnership assigns well-defined meanings to its bids and bidding sequences.
TABLE PRESENCE:	The ability to draw inferences from the extraneous things that happen at the table.
TAKEOUT DOUBLE:	Double that requests partner not to pass but to choose a suit (or notrump) to play in.
TEMPORIZE:	Bid a suit (often, an unplayable suit), in the expectation of supporting partner's suit later. May be required if no immediate raise is appropriate.
TENACE:	An honor or combination of honors which will be most valuable if the holder is fourth-hand to play; e.g., AQ, KJ.
THIRD HAND:	In the auction, dealer's partner. In the play, leader's partner.
THIRD-SEAT OPENING:	An opening bid after two passes that may be based on sub-minimum values. Often it is intended as mainly lead-directing and mildly preemptive.

THROW-IN:	See ENDPLAY.
TRAP PASS:	Pass made with substantial values, including strength in the opponent's suit, in the hope of making a successful penalty double later.
TREATMENT:	A particular way of assigning a natural meaning to a bid or sequence of bids.
TRICK:	Four cards played in sequence, one by each player at the table, going clockwise.
TRUMPS:	The suit determined in the bidding to be that of the contract.
TRUMP CONTROL:	Technique by which declarer makes possession of the trump suit work to his advantage, exhausting the opponents of their trumps so he can safely establish and cash other winners.
TRUMP COUP:	The advanced play by which declarer can avoid losing a trick to an outstanding trump honor by forcing the defender to ruff and be overruffed.
TRUMP ECHO:	The high-low sequence of play in the trump suit, used in defense to show an odd number of trumps.
TRUMP PROMOTION:	Defensive technique in which declarer is forced to either ruff low and be overruffed or ruff high at the later cost of a trick.
TRUMP SUPPORT:	Usually four or more cards in partner's suit. Under some circumstances, three or fewer cards.
UNBALANCED HAND:	Hand containing a void suit or singleton.
UNBLOCK:	Play by declarer or defenders so as to allow the uninterrupted run of a long suit by proper management of the smaller cards.
UNDERTRICKS:	Tricks which declarer has bid but fails to take.
UPPERCUT:	Defensive technique in which a defender ruffs in with a trump intermediate and declarer is obliged to weaken his trump holding by overruffing.
VOID:	A suit in which no cards are held.
VULNERABILITY:	Condition in the scoring, achieved when one game has been won toward completion of the rubber.
WEAK TWO-BID:	Modern treatment in which an opening bid of 2♠, 2♡ or 2◇ shows a good six-card suit and about an average hand in high cards.

What the Proprieties Are About:

In a game such as poker, all sorts of at-the-table gamesmanship is allowed. In bridge, *skill in choosing a bid or play is emphasized.* A strict code of ethics and courtesy is part of the game. The better the players in the game, the higher the standard of ethics is likely to be. A higher standard of ethics is demanded in tournament play than in a social game at home. The purpose of the *Proprieties,* that section of the Laws of bridge that deals with conduct and ethics, is to make the game more enjoyable for everyone, no matter what the situation.

Please take time to read these excerpts from the Proprieties, as taken from the Laws of Duplicate Contract Bridge. If you observe the principles set down here, you will find yourself respected as both a partner and an opponent.

Conduct and Etiquette:

A player should maintain at all times a courteous attitude toward his partner and the opponents. He should carefully avoid any remark or action that might cause annoyance or embarrassment to another player, or that might interfere with another player's enjoyment of the game.

As a matter of courtesy, a play should refrain from:

Paying insufficient attention;
Making gratuitous comments during the play as to the auction or the adequacy of the contract;
Detaching a card from his hand before it is his turn to play;
Arranging the cards he has played to previous tricks in a disorderly manner or mixing his cards together before the result of the deal has been agreed to;
Making a questionable claim or concession; or
Prolonging the play unnecessarily.

It is a breach of the Proprieties to:

Use different designations for the same call ("A Club," "I'll bid a club," etc., are incorrect. "One club" is the only proper form).
Indicate any approval or disapproval of a call or play.

188

Indicate the expectation or intention of winning or losing a
trick before play to that trick has been completed.

Comment or act during the auction or play to call attention
to a significant incident thereof, or to the state of the
score, or to the number of tricks that will be required
for success.

Look intently at any other player during the auction or
play, or at another player's hand for the purpose of seeing his cards or observing the place from which he
draws a card.

Vary the normal tempo of bidding or play for the purpose
of disconcerting the other players.

Communication Between Partners:

Communication between partners during the auction and play
should be effected only by means of the calls and plays themselves.
Calls should be made in a uniform tone without special emphasis
or inflection, and without undue haste or hesitation. Plays should
be made without emphasis, gesture or mannerism, and so far as possible, at a uniform rate.

It is improper for communication between partners to be effected
through the *manner* in which calls and plays are made, through ex-
traneous remarks or gestures, or through questions asked of the opponents or explanations given to them. When a player has available
to him improper information from his partner's remark, question,
explanation, gesture, mannerism, special emphasis, inflection, haste
or hesitation, *he should carefully avoid taking any advantage that
might accrue to his side.*

If it is determined that a player chose from among logical alternative actions one that could reasonably have been suggested by his
partner's tempo, manner or remark, and this results in damage to
innocent opponents, the score on the deal should be adjusted in favor
of the innocent side. (Such an outcome *by no means implies* that the
side that committed an infraction did so *deliberately.* The very problem with, say, hesitations, is that it is almost impossible for a player's
objectivity not to be clouded by the fact that his partner has huddled.
Who can say that he will not be *subconsciously* influenced by the
huddle? Therefore, it is common practice today to routinely give
redress to the innocent side in such situations.)

It is improper to have special understandings with partner regard-
ing your bids and play of which the opponents are unaware. The op-

ponents are entitled to know about that fancy new bidding Convention you and partner had decided to try out, and you are obliged to announce it to them before the game starts.

The Laws prescribe no formal penalty for violating any of the *Proprieties*. However, players who are careless and get to be known for a low standard of ethics will find that fewer and fewer players are willing to play with them.

A Note on Partnership Rapport:

There are many bridge players who look on partner as a necessary evil, but your success at the bridge table will depend in great part

AVOID CRITICIZING YOUR PARTNER.

on how well your partner performs. *Everything* that happens within your partnership can affect what kind of results you get, so your partner's morale should be important to you.

Nobody likes harsh criticism under any circumstances, but for people who play bridge seriously, the game is a real ego trip. We are sensitive about our game and our mistakes. If you point out your partner's errors right at the table (or, worse, if you are downright abusive), you are unlikely to accomplish anything constructive. On the contrary, you will probably get partner to dwell on his errors and induce him to play even worse.

A partnership at bridge is two people trying to act as one in an emotionally-charged setting. Recognize that when one player criticizes his partner, it is because he views partner's error as a direct reflection on his own ability; his sensitivity has been ruffled.

You should always assume that your partner wants to win as badly as you do, and he is trying as hard as he can. Therefore, withhold any criticism until after the game. Instead, you should be interested in *building* up his ego. If he makes an error, tell him that you would probably have done the same thing under the circumstances; or that he probably had what he thought was a good reason at the time he made his misguided bid or play. Give his ego a chance to recover and he will play harder for the rest of the game.

Do your partner, your partnership and yourself a favor. Apply the Golden Rule when your partner makes an error.

DEVYN PRESS PUBLICATIONS
BRIDGE BOOKS